MANY FORMS OF MADNESS

A Family's Struggle with Mental Illness and the Mental Health System

Rosemary Radford Ruether

With David Ruether

Fortress Press

Minneapolis

MANY FORMS OF MADNESS
A Family's Struggle with Mental Illness and the Mental Health System

Cover image: "Profile of a man's head with a spotlight on his brain." Bull's Eye/ ImageZoo Illustration Disc: *Targeting Health*. Royalty free.
Cover design: Laurie Ingram
Book design: PerfecType, Nashville, TN
Photos courtesy of Rosemary Radford Ruether and David Ruether

Library of Congress Cataloging-in-Publication Data
Ruether, Rosemary Radford.
  Many forms of madness : a family's struggle with mental illness and the mental health system / Rosemary Radford Ruether ; with David Ruether.
    p. cm.
  Includes bibliographical references and index.
  ISBN 978-0-8006-9651-1
  1. Ruether, David, 1959—Mental health. 2. Schizophrenics—California— Biography. 3. Schizophrenics—Family relationships. 4. Mental illness— Treatment—United States. I. Ruether, David, 1959– II. Title.
  RC514.R84 2010
  616.89'80092—dc22
  [B]

                                                        2009042225

The paper used in this publication meets the minimum requirements of American National Standard for Information Sciences—Permanence of Paper for Printed Library Materials, ANSI Z329.48-1984.
Manufactured in the U.S.A.

14 13 12 11 10   1 2 3 4 5 6 7 8 9 10

MANY FORMS OF MADNESS

"*Many Forms of Madness* is an intriguing, gripping account of personal and family pain around a loved one's need and the society's failure to provide help. This is a must read for persons and families dealing with the mental health system and for pastoral/spiritual caregivers caring for them. This work gives a candid view of the ways in which these needs are not adequately being met and suggests ways in which changes could be made to improve care."

> Teresa E. Snorton
> Executive Director
> Association for Clinical Pastoral Education, Inc.

Contents

Acknowledgments

I wish to thank Bob and Laura Fukada who read and commented on this manuscript from their experience. I thank Pete Sabey, a practicing family therapist, and Jim Poling, of the Garrett-Evangelical Theological Seminary Pastoral Counseling Department, who gave the manuscript a careful reading from their long experience in the family therapy and pastoral psychology fields. I thank Kathleen Greider of the Claremont School of Theology Pastoral Care and Counseling Department for helpful advice and the loan of many of her books in the research for this book. I thank Dick Bunce who gave a critical reading of several chapters from the perspective of his long history with the Mental Health system of Los Angeles County. I thank Theresa Yugar and Diane Ward, doctoral students at the Claremont Graduate University, who read and commented on the manuscript from their personal experiences. Finally I thank Mary Elizabeth Ruether and Rebecca Ruether who read the manuscript from the perspective of their own history with their brother. Finally I thank Herman Ruether, faithful companion in this journey, who read and commented on this entire manuscript.

Introduction

I am writing this book for and with my son, David Christopher Ruether. It represents our almost thirty years of struggle with his mental illness that has debilitated him since his late teens. It also is about our struggle as parents with the mental health system in the United States, as we have pursued our son through his vicissitudes of hospitals, nursing homes, and board-and-care homes in the search for better advice and better treatment for his illness.

I have folded David's personal story into the story of the changing face of how those with mental illness have been treated in the United States, from colonial times to the present. I brought in this historical context not only because I am a historian and deeply interested in how ideas and practices have developed historically but also—and more importantly—because of my realization of how little has changed in the treatment of those with mental illness.

The usual view of the history of the treatment of those with mental illness is that while there may have been some barbaric treatment in the past, it has now been overcome. The development of psychotropic drugs and the emptying of mental hospitals in the 1950s to 1970s signaled the dawn of enlightened treatment of these people. It is said that society now realizes that this illness is simply a physical disease like any other; it is treatable with medications, and those who suffer from it can live as valued members of society. However, the reality of the situation is very different. In fact, Americans have gone from one inhumane solution to another for persons with mental illness. Today, the incarceration of many of those with mental illness has been transferred from mental hospitals to jails. The worse descriptions of the bedlam of prisons and mental hospitals in the eighteenth or nineteenth centuries, where people were chained to their beds, shouting or mute, naked and idle, lying in their own excrement, can now be duplicated in the pretrial mental wards of county jails.[1]

Tragically, each of the shifts has been accompanied by great waves of reform led by idealistic reformers determined to rescue those with mental illness from abusive situations and give them a truly humane and dignified life. So what has gone wrong with these reforms? Why do we as a family with a son with mental illness struggle with such poor alternatives today? Answering these questions is an integral part of the story contained here. It also tries to envision better alternatives, to imagine what our society would do for those with mental illness "if we really cared," and it presents some examples of groups who are doing a better job.

This book is primarily the fruit of my research and writing, but it is also an expression of a family collaboration. Herman Ruether has been a central part of this struggle with David's mental illness over the years, and he has been a constant consultant on this book, reading and discussing all its chapters. David has also been an integral part, not only because it is his story but also because his own experiences, thoughts, and writings have been brought in at many points. I have consulted him on many issues and at times have quoted verbatim some of our conversations. His own writings play an important role in the narrative. This book seeks to make David's voice heard. His two sisters have also played a role by reading major parts of the manuscript and giving me feedback and sharing how they want their own experiences represented.

I wish to say a word about terminology in this book. I have avoided the terms *the mentally ill* or *a mentally ill person* since they seem to essentialize mental illness as the identity of the person. Just as we would not refer to a person with cancer as a cancerous person, so we should not refer to a person with mental illness as a mentally ill person. I have adopted a number of ways of referring to different individuals and groups with mental illness in terms of the context. In the traditional hospital for persons suffering from mental illness, the term *patient* seems appropriate. I occasionally use words like *maniac*, *crazy*, and *insane*, but only as references to past historical usage, and usually in quotes. Several movements, such as Thresholds and the Village, see themselves as communities and call the people who participate in their movement *members*, while Gould Farm refers to them as *guests*, so I use these terms in the context of these movements.

Mostly I just use the term *persons* in varying contexts, such as "persons with mental illness" or "persons receiving mental health services." I do not use the term *consumer*, which is favored by the National Alliance on Mental Illness. To me, *consumer* is market terminology. It refers to someone who buys goods and consumes products. What are people with mental illness being presumed to "buy" or "consume"? Mental health services? Medications? I think this term masks the involuntary way that medications are being imposed, for the most part, and the underlying medical model that still shapes this relationship.

This book unfolds in six chapters. The first chapter consists of an overview of David's life from birth in 1959 to the time of the completion of this writing in March 2009. It is organized around six periods: early childhood in the Claremont area of southern California; his youth in Washington, D.C.; young adulthood (with some months spent in Cambridge, England, and then in Evanston, Illinois) and the early onset of schizophrenia; the eight years he spent in Hawaii from 1987 to 1995; the period from 1995 to 2002, when he returned to the Chicago area and bounced around between various hospitals, nursing homes, and board-and-care homes; and the most recent period in which he, with us, his parents, returned to the Claremont, California, area.

This biographical chapter was originally written to help psychiatrists and social workers understand the different aspects and stages of David's experience with mental illness and the mental health system in the context of his larger life experience. Except for one director of a local clinic, I have never met a social worker or psychiatrist interested in reading it. Apparently, these professional roles can be carried out without understanding very much about the person whom one is "treat-ing." I have expanded this biography to put everything else in the book in the context of David's own experience of mental illness and the men-tal health system over the last thirty years.

The second chapter details the symptoms of schizophrenia as defined by the DSM, the *Diagnostic and Statistical Manual of Mental Disorders*, the official manual published by the American Psychiatric Association to diagnose mental illness. The chapter compares these symptoms with David's experience with such phenomena as voices, obsessions and paranoia, incoherent speech and thought, and passivity or lack of motivation. It traces the overlap of much of such phenomena with "normal" human experience and explores the problematic labeling of such experiences as "illness" caused by a "brain defect." The hearing of voices and visual hallucinations is discussed in terms of their widespread appearance in religious experience, both in the origins and ongoing expe-rience of Christianity and also in Islam and in African-Latin American religions, such as Santeria and Condomblé. It compares David's verbally rich and complex writings with the theories of "incoherent speech" and "poverty of thought" in the DSM diagnosis. Finally, it asks how much of the patterns of passivity and lack of motivation are manifestations of an illness and how much is medication induced and socialized through a mental health system of care designed to produce dependency.

The third chapter traces the pattern of continual oscillation and ten-sion between mental-psychological theories and somatic theories of the causes of schizophrenia. It looks at these conflicting views in three his-torical stages in Western (especially American) culture: (1) the Christian and classical views inherited by colonial America that saw mental illness alternatively as caused by demonic possession, on the one hand, and by the imbalance of the humors of the body, on the other; (2) the drift between "moral treatment" in the early asylum movement in the early nineteenth century and the increasing focus on somatic causes or "brain lesions" and on somatic treatments like hydrotherapy, shock treatments, and lobotomy that continued into the mid-twentieth century; and (3) the Freudian psychoanalysis and the antipsychiatry movement of the 1960s that challenged these somatic theories and treatments but was followed by a return with a vengeance to purely somatic or "chemical" theories of the defective brain and a preference for drug treatment of mental illness to the virtual exclusion of any "talk" therapy in contemporary psychiatric theory and practice. The chapter also discuss several new developments of thought that question the mind-body dualism underlying this opposition of mental-psychic versus somatic theories. It lifts up the need to see the interaction of mind and brain, the social and the somatic. It concludes with some of David's own reflections on the causes of his "problems."

The fourth chapter asks why those with mental illness have so often been treated so violently and abusively, based on assumptions of what is good for them. It suggests that part of this abusive treatment lies in the need to separate ourselves as "normal" and "rational" from those with mental illness, to deny the continuity between us, and to repress our fears of those "others" as potentially "us." It sketches the history of abusive treatment from chaining, beating, and extreme neglect in prison-like hospitals or "bedlams" to the shock treatments and lobotomies that became favored in the early to mid-twentieth century, and takes up the question of the new neuroleptic medications developed from the 1950s and the increasing use of them for more and more categories of human experience pathologized as "mental illness." The chapter also explores the work of Peter Breggin, a psychiatrist whose writings and legal activism have challenged the reign of the chemicalization of treatment of psychic experience, including that of younger and younger children, in preference for any tradition of guidance in a "soul journey" toward maturity and wisdom. This questioning of the reign of "meds" includes a brief exploration of the way in which the psychiatric establishment is being corrupted by big money through drug companies. I conclude by reflecting on our own dilemmas as a family trying to make our way in the midst of this cacophony of conflicting voices about what to do.

Chapter 5, on living arrangements, addresses not just physical housing but the various environments that our societies, from colonial times to the present, have set up for the domiciling of those with mental illness. The chapter addresses the vision of moral treatment that arose in response to the abusive treatment of those with mental illness in prisons, asylums, and poorhouses in the late eighteenth and early nineteenth centuries. The development of moral treatment by the Quakers at the Retreat in York, England, an institution that still exists, is discussed in some detail. How this vision of moral treatment deteriorated into the new snake pit of the state mental hospital from the mid-nineteenth to the mid-twentieth centuries is then discussed. The last half of the chapter focuses on the critique and emptying of the state mental hospitals in the 1960s and 1970s as a result of a new reform movement that favored "community care." It discusses how this movement—what has been called "deinstitutionalization"—has deteriorated into the relegation of those with mental illness to a new set of inhumane institutions, the nursing home, and the board-and-care home. Many of those who would formerly have been hospitalized are now found in the street as homeless people or in the jail.

The last chapter seeks to provide some vision of an alternative to this grim picture. It details four much-more-adequate and hopeful therapeutic communities and movements that David and we, his parents, have experienced over the last twenty-five years: the Duck Island experiment, Gould Farm, Kahumana, and Threshholds. It also discusses a fifth very helpful effort to provide an integrated network of services for those with mental illness in Long Beach, California: The Village, with its focus on recovery, not just maintenance. This perusal of more hopeful alternatives with a real vision of recovery is followed by an effort to imagine what a more adequate system of mental health services might look like. I speculate on how we might bring together the hospital, housing, and the community clinic, with work, education, recreation, and social life organized on the county level.

Finally, the book concludes with a brief reflection on what a *spirituality for recovery* might mean both for advocates and for those struggling with mental illness. How do we commit ourselves to long-term advocacy for someone with mental illness and not overwhelm our own lives? How do those with mental illness nurture ongoing hope and not be overwhelmed with sadness for all that has been lost? The chapter ends with a poem by David on the journey through the "storm" and back to the "light."

1

David's Life and Hard and (Sometimes) Good Times

David Christopher Ruether was born at Pomona Hospital in Pomona, California, on December 6, 1959. My husband, Herman, and I were both graduate students at the Claremont Graduate School at the time. Two things stand out for me about David's birth. The first is that the doctor induced labor, because David was not being born quickly enough, and he circumcised David without asking our permission. These procedures bothered me because I wondered whether the drugs used to induce labor might injure the baby and because it had not occurred to me that it was the practice in American hospitals to circumcise male babies without asking permission of the parents. The other thing that stands out for me is how excited Herman was at the birth. I remember watching his head bobbing up and down in the window of the delivery room door as he eagerly tried to catch a glimpse of his newborn child.

I named David for my uncle David Sandow, husband of my paternal aunt. David Sandow was from the Jewish tradition, a musician and artist who had been a surrogate father for my sisters and me while our father was in Europe during the Second World War. David, who had no children of his own, was our mentor in music and the fine arts. Naming my son after Uncle David was a way of honoring this relationship. Years

later, while executing my aunt's estate, I was touched to discover that
Uncle David had cherished a picture I had given him of our David as a
blond, rosy-cheeked two-year-old.

Early Childhood, 1959–1966

David is the middle child in our family. His older sister, Becky, is twenty
months older and his younger sister, Mimi, three years and three
months younger. We lived in Claremont, California, when our children
were preschoolers. I had a teaching-assistant position at Scripps College, which was paying for my tuition in Claremont Graduate School.
Herman taught at California Polytechnic College in Pomona. A Mexican woman cared for the children during the hours I was in class. She
was a motherly woman, and I remember her settling into a rocking
chair with David on her ample bosom as I ran out to class. Later, Jo
Verich, a good friend with three children of her own about the same
age as mine, took care of David and his sisters while I was in school.
They enjoyed playing with their Verich friends during the hours I was
away each morning.

By the time David was three, we had purchased a home in South
Claremont, a former orange grove ranch house that had been moved to
a pleasant neighborhood. There was a garden in the front of the house
and a large covered patio in the back. Many a child's birthday party took
place on that patio. Much time was also spent at the Claremont Park in
the wading pool and playing on the merry-go-round and swings. Becky
was athletic, and David was hard put to keep up with his older sister on
the swings and gym bars or when riding bicycles.

When David was five years old, he began kindergarten at St. Paul's
Episcopal School in Pomona. Starting school apparently awakened
some tension in David, which was expressed in some new behaviors. To
my surprise, he became a bit of a playground terror and got into a few
fights during recess. I also remember that he developed a tic, in which
he would jerk his head nervously. I tried to get him to stop, and after a
few months he eventually did.

During this time one of our favorite things to do was visit the Barnes household in nearby La Verne. Kate Barnes, a graduate of Scripps College, was a poet married to a Pomona College professor of English. The Barnes had four children and they owned a large property in the foothills where Kate raised horses. There was also a swimming pool on the property. Long, lazy afternoons were spent riding the horses, traveling the foothill trails in a horse and buggy, or swimming in the pool. Another favorite excursion was to La

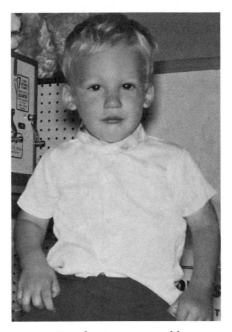

David as a two-year-old

Jolla, California, to visit my mother, who had a charming house with orange trees in the backyard that was located two blocks from "Wind and Sea" beach. We would drive or take the train there for weekends or summer holidays, and we would wander the beautiful beaches and elegant shops of this seaside resort town. During the summer of 1965, at the height of the civil rights struggle, I volunteered with Delta Ministry in Mississippi while my three children enjoyed a pleasant summer with my mother in La Jolla.

Washington Years, 1966–1975

In the summer of 1966, we moved to Washington, D.C. I had completed my Ph.D. and had accepted a part-time teaching position at George Washington University and a part-time position at the Howard University School of Religion. Herman had a teaching position at American

University School of International Service. We rented a three-story town house in the Arlington Heights area of Washington, D.C.

School and Church Communities

That fall David began first grade and Becky second at the local Catholic parochial school on Sixteenth Street. The nuns were authoritarian and, I learned, accustomed to hitting children with rulers. It also very soon became apparent to me that they mourned that the clientele of their school was changing from upper-class whites to middle-class and poor blacks; they expressed joy in having the Ruethers add a couple of white children to the student body. Being very much involved in the civil rights movement, I was sensitized to and offended by their racism. Although David was only six years old, he too remembers these nuns as "mean." One day I stopped by the school during recess and found my son and daughter huddled under the school steps, while the other children shouted and rushed around. I took David and Becky out of the school and transferred them to a private school on the Wisconsin Avenue side of town.

We found a worshiping community in St. Stephen and the Incarnation Episcopal Church, which had an ecumenical membership and a strong civil rights and peace orientation. The liturgies reflected a liberation theology approach, and many civil rights and antiwar protest movements had their staging areas at St. Stephen's. Fourteenth Street, which ran next to the church, was the major corridor for burning and looting during the riots in Washington that followed the assassination of Martin Luther King Jr. in 1968. On Palm Sunday, after the end of the riots, parishioners marched down Fourteenth Street, placing flowers in the barrels of guns held by the troops that lined both sides of the street.

David grew up in this activist church from the ages of seven to thirteen, and was good friends with Andrew Wendt, son of the pastor, William Wendt. David participated in civil rights and antiwar marches, picketed the White House, and on several Good Fridays walked in

Stations of the Cross processions that wound through official Washington, identifying various sites of global injustice as places where Christ had been crucified that year. We knew the Berrigan brothers, Daniel and Phil, and their followers. Mary Moylan, one of the Catonsville Nine who, in 1973, poured blood on draft files in Catonsville, Maryland, was a close friend and neighbor whose home was a place of frequent social action gatherings.

In 1968 we bought a home in the upper Sixteenth Street area. David and Andrew Wendt both attended the local public school in the third and fourth grades. David's sister Becky remembers this as a fun neighborhood, with lots of kids to play with, but also a tough environment, where bikes and bags were stolen often. Later, I moved both David and Becky to a parent-run school near Catholic University, attended by the children of middle-class Washington professionals. Our children were among the few white students and they became accustomed to being with Asian and African American classmates who were smart and competitive.

David could read before beginning first grade and thus was allowed to start first grade early. He also skipped seventh grade. This was a mistake in my opinion, because it pushed him ahead of his age group. Due to this accelerated pace, David graduated from primary school in 1972, the same year as his older sister.

Trying Teen Years

In 1972–1973 I was a visiting lecturer at Harvard Divinity School in Cambridge, Massachusetts. We lived in a working-class neighborhood just north of the city. David and Becky went to a Catholic parochial high school with very progressive nuns. The students were mostly children of working-class Boston Catholics. Unfortunately, they conceived a prejudice against David as a Southerner. It had never occurred to me to think of my children as Southerners, but having grown up in Washington, D.C., their accents sounded "southern" to the ears of Bostonians. David was also "pretty" and wore his hair in shoulder-length light brown curls, which perhaps also aroused their prejudice. These experiences wounded David's budding sense of his masculinity, but he did find a home at the local YMCA where he became an outstanding member of the swim team.

Another much deeper wound to David's psyche occurred two years later when he was fifteen. At the time we were vaguely aware that a middle-aged gay male couple lived in a large corner house in our neighborhood, but neither Herman nor I ever met them. Sometime in the year before we left Washington, one of these men lured David into his house and either exposed himself to David or committed a sexual act with him; it is not clear to us what actually happened. We first learned of this incident during one of David's hospitalizations years later, when he broke down in tears and told us about it. David had been harboring a deep sense of shame over this incident since his mid-teens.

We returned to Washington at the conclusion of my visiting lectureship at Harvard. David attended Gongaza, the Jesuit high school in D.C., his sophomore, junior, and senior years. He was a middling student, prone to conflicts with the Jesuits and constantly judged as not working up to his potential. I tended to defend him, thinking that these were normal growing pains that would resolve themselves in the post high school years. There was no evidence of mental illness, at least not that we could notice, and it did not occur to us that this might be a possibility.

David and Becky's close friends, many of whom were the offspring of Washington professionals, were into drugs, mostly smoking marijuana. We didn't know the extent of their drug use, nor what effect being in this drug culture had on David. He did not seem to us to have a drug problem, but evidently he was much more attracted to the "highs" that drugs promised than we realized.

David's reflective turn of mind at the age of fifteen is expressed in a short poem he wrote after a long, hot drive in the family car across the desert from Mexico to California:

"The Desert"

Is the weather so hot I cannot feel? Think?
The mind floats,
Concentration and comprehension are gone.
I lie in the back seat in an oblivious state.
Will it never end?
This cooped-up-ness?
I want to be active,
Not a vegetable to be cooked by the elements
In a square tin box.

Death is outside the window.
The graves created by a harsh environment,
Waiting for another victim,
Waiting for yet another being
To be rendered useless,
Another bone to bleach,
More metal to rust.

This is god's wasteland,
Though it is graced by beauty and wonder,
By unparalleled spectacles of vision.
It is never-the-less forsaken,
The Devil's playground,
Which God has set aside for his alter ego
And for those who are strong enough
In spirit to rend the veil of civilized illusion
And gaze naked into her stark reality.

Chicago Years, 1976–1987

Both Becky and David graduated from high school in 1976. David was sixteen. I had been offered a theological chair at the Garrett Theological Seminary in Evanston, Illinois, so we made plans to sell our house and move to the Chicago area. We looked forward to moving away from Washington to extricate our children from their circle of friends, many of whom were now heavily into drugs. Since we felt that David was too

David at sixteen: Graduation from Gonzaga High School, Washington, D.C.

young and immature to go on to college, we decided to send him to a preparatory college in Cambridge, England, where the daughter of a colleague had spent a year after graduating from high school. A year abroad seemed like a good idea for David's development. The son of a first cousin was also a student at Cambridge University, so David would have a family contact there.

We drove from Washington to Chicago in two cars: my husband, our younger daughter, and I in our van, and David, then a competent driver, piloting our orange Volkswagen with his older sister as passenger. I still remember David's and Becky's proud, smiling faces looking out the window at us as we drove parallel along the highways.

David headed off to England in the autumn of 1976, but the stay at Cambridgeshire College did not go well. He was registered for English, Spanish, history, and psychology, but he attended little to his schoolwork. Among the students were a group of wealthy boys from Turkey and other Middle East countries who smoked hash. Other students with whom David associated also used pot, and LSD was available as well. David dropped acid at least twice, going berserk and riding around in cabs and running up and down stairs in the YMCA where he was living. In January his advisor told him and us that he should leave. He returned home to Evanston in early February.

Something Is Wrong with David

Mimi, David's younger sister, remembers that she felt immediately upon David's return from England that there was something wrong with him. She sensed that David was acting "different," although she can't name exactly how.

In the spring of 1977, we endeavored to have David start school at a local community college, but he was unable to concentrate. On the theory that perhaps he needed more time to "get himself together," we allowed him to go off to Cuernavaca, Mexico, for part of the summer to study Spanish.

David was familiar with Cuernavaca because we had spent summers there as a family when he was in his earlier teens. David had taken Spanish in high school, and during his time in Cuernavaca he became fairly fluent in the language, writing letters and even poems in Spanish. David had another major achievement during this time, too. Along with a friend, David climbed Mount Popocatepetal, the snow-clad peak that borders Mexico City. This is a feat that he still cherishes.

David was scheduled to return from Mexico in the latter part of the summer to attend summer school at Santa Cruz University. In preparation for this, he had stayed with his grandmother in La Jolla, California, before going to Cuernavaca, and had used the time to study for college entrance exams. He had taken the exams, with success, at San Diego High School before heading to Mexico. But David's time in Mexico was cut short. He had been in Cuernavaca only a month when we got a call from an acquaintance of his alerting us to the fact that David was wandering around incoherently and shouldn't be there on his own. David returned to California, managing the bus ride on his own, but his plan to attend summer school in Santa Cruz fell apart disastrously. Unable to concentrate in class, David took to walking around the area instead. On one occasion the campus police found him walking on a wall, and told him to get down. There was a verbal exchange and David apparently made an insulting comment in Spanish, which one police officer understood. David was arrested and jailed, even though there were no charges. Herman drove to California, and David was released into his father's custody, with orders not to return to California for a year.

David was sullen during the ride home with his father. Herman says that David often glanced at him angrily, and he sensed hostility in David, something he had not previously observed. Yet David also seemed to have no idea what he would do without his parents. At one point Herman said to him, "You know, we won't live forever. What will you do when we are gone?" David replied, "I guess I will just curl up and die."

During the next year David lived in our home in Evanston, and we witnessed periodic bouts of violence, coupled with vituperation. He particularly targeted his father, throwing out vicious comments that deprecated Herman's entire humanity and all his interests. In one fight David sent a blow to his father's face that broke his glasses. On other occasions the houses in which we lived bore the brunt of David's violence: a gate broken, the door to our bedroom shattered, a chandelier in the dining room smashed. Once when Herman and I were away and David was home alone with his younger sister, David went into a rage, throwing books and destroying the rungs of the stairs leading up from the basement.

By now David was six feet four and his physical capacity was beyond our control. A friend who was in medical school visited us during this period and reported with alarm a "word salad" pattern of thought in David's speech, which she identified as characteristic of schizophrenia.

We began a round of visits to therapists, first attending family therapy in a local hospital and then consulting with therapists who focused on David. We also began to call the police when David became violent, and, as a result, he was taken to psychiatric wards of several local hospitals. After a stay of usually two weeks, David would come home calmed, but eventually the cycle would begin again.

We struggled to help David pursue school or employment of some kind. At one time or another he managed to hold down jobs providing room service at the Orrington Hotel in Evanston, washing dishes in a local college cafeteria, and cleaning up the town park, but in each case the job lasted only for a month or two. We connected David with a tutor.

We also helped him sign up for a distance-learning course, which he was able to complete with a lot of encouragement from us.

Finding a Place for David

Eventually it became evident to Herman and me that we could not allow David to continue living in our house. It seemed only a matter of time before he would do something that would result in serious injury to one or more of us. The tension and danger that David brought to our daily lives seriously jeopardized our ability to keep up with our teaching responsibilities and the additional writing and lecturing I was doing. His younger sister, then in high school, needed a calm family environment.

We began to search for a therapeutic community that would accept David. Our hope was to find a place in the country with outdoor activity, since it seemed to us that the best thing for David was to be physically busy, with organized work and recreation. In a handbook of intentional communities we found several interesting options.

The first place we arranged for David to live was off the coast of Maine. Duck Island was an experimental therapeutic community organized by a somewhat maverick Doctor Cloutier, who was critical of the standard psychiatric approach to treating of schizophrenics with drugs. David was there for a little more than two months, and he remembers it as one of the most positive experiences of his long career with care facilities. Living on Duck Island required vigorous physical activity. All supplies were brought over from the mainland by boat. These had to be purchased in regular trips and then loaded onto the boat in high surf, rowed to the island, and unloaded. David seemed to thrive with this physical activity. He also walked around the island daily and wrote a good deal of poetry and other reflections. Unfortunately, Doctor Cloutier did not have the means to keep the community running. Duck Island closed at the end of the summer and David returned to Chicago.

During the next year we experimented with care facilities in the Chicago area. David was very resistant to them and clearly felt threatened by the typical psychiatric board-and-care housing. On one occasion, as Herman and I were getting ready to leave after settling David into his new residence, David made a move as if to jump out of a second-story window. David did stay some months at a residence called Squire's House, which looked a bit like a motel and provided little besides a room and food service. But he frequently walked home, some twenty miles from downtown Chicago, putting us in a position of having to drive him back to the residence.

We continued to search information sources on alternative communities and eventually found another therapeutic community, this one in western Massachusetts. Gould Farm agreed to take David in the fall of 1984.

Gould Farm was a much more established place than Duck Island, having been in business for many years. There were many more residents and a full staff. The activities consisted of farm work, grounds maintenance, and food preparation, as well as opportunities for education and physical recreation. The philosophy was one of a highly organized—even regimented—day with regular hours of work. The expectation was that if one could operate within this supervised regimentation, one could prepare for independence; there were work opportunities within the community (a store, a restaurant) to which a person might graduate.

David was put on the food preparation team, having held jobs before in this kind of work. But he typically got up late and missed breakfast, and so was relegated to dishwashing. By late fall David was having conflicts with staff demands, and by Christmas, following a fight with another patient, he was sent home. We were paying for David's stay at Gould Farm, and the costs were becoming prohibitive for us.

After another two years of David moving back and forth between our home and care homes or hospitals, and meeting with therapists, we again began to search for a therapeutic community that would provide David with work and regimen. We also explored the theory promoted by one of David's therapists that schizophrenia might be caused by certain vitamin and mineral deficiencies. A clinic near Princeton, New Jersey, did tests and prescribed a regimen of vitamins and minerals. We took David for these tests and put him on these supplements. It is not clear whether it was of any help.

David Hears Multiple Voices

By this time, David was plagued heavily by multiple voices—male and female—that he seemed to think were coming from radio and television but were broadcast to him personally. These voices, in so far as he was able to discuss them, seemed primarily to demean him, telling him he was worthless. Our constant efforts to explain to him that these were his own inner voices and that he should reject their messages and affirm his worth were of little avail. David experienced the voices as something outside of himself that bombarded him.

These voices prompted some of David's bouts of rage, usually directed at another patient whom he "heard" saying negative things about him or members of his family. Several times he struck others because he heard them demeaning his beloved grandmother (who by this time was dead and whom the offenders had never met). Medications never seemed to have the slightest effect on diminishing David's voices.

Hawaii Years: 1987–1995

In 1987 we discovered Kahumana, an interesting therapeutic community in the Hawaiian Islands. Kahumana was begun in downtown Honolulu by an ecumenical alliance working with people with mental illness. The group consisted of a Catholic nun with a psychiatric practice, a priest ordained in an Eastern rite Catholic church, and a group of related people who belonged to the Anthroposophical tradition, which is well-known for its alternative school system.

After establishing their ministry in the city of Honolulu, the group decided to relocate to a more rural setting. They bought property in Waianae on the north end of the island of Oahu and established a community with extensive fruit orchards, a chicken-raising project, and meditative gardens. Residences were built for the nun and the priest, and attractive community buildings in a native Hawaiian style were constructed for the residents, who consisted of a small community of "patients" together with the families of the Anthroposophical group.

Kahumana offered opportunities for several kinds of spirituality and religious services, including an Eastern rite mass, but there was no pressure to participate in any of these religious activities.

In the summer of 1987, we took David to Kahumana, loaded with his regimen of vitamins and minerals. He settled into a pleasant room in one of the patient residences. An activity director got David involved in riding and grooming horses. She also signed him up for membership at a local athletic club, where he played tennis regularly. A mile walk brought him to a beautiful cove and beach where he swam.

David was willing to help care for the orchards, and he was put in charge of caring for the chickens, which involved carrying out the vegetable and fruit scraps from the meals, mixing them with grain, and scattering the mix among the chickens. David enjoyed these tasks and worked at them consistently. The director praised David for his initiative when many other patients preferred to lie about in their rooms and watch television. We called David weekly and every six or eight months planned a trip to visit him for a few days.

The first year at Kahumana went very well, but in the second year both David and the community deteriorated. While jogging back from the beach, David was hit by a car and though not badly hurt, he was bruised and shaken up. The activity director and her horses disappeared. The priest gathered around him several young male staff, which David seemed to find threatening. We have no evidence that there was any actual misconduct by this priest, but there was a certain "gay male" ambiance that was upsetting to David, and soon he was fighting with them. By the end of the second year, David was expelled from Kahumana and placed with the mental health system of the state of Hawaii.

David's Sexuality

It is appropriate at this point to say something about David's sexuality. The nun at Kahumana suggested to us that David was homosexual and that his strong homophobia reflected his denial of this. Although we would not rule out this possibility (and are not against healthy gay relationships), we were inclined to reject this judgment. We have many

David in Hawaii at thirty-five, c. 1994

gay male and lesbian friends who are mature adults in good sexual, mostly monogamous, relationships. These friends consistently report that they knew they were homosexual because from their early teens they were spontaneously physically attracted to people of the same sex. Same-sex attraction also filled their fantasy lives. Even though most were socialized to fight these attractions and to feel ashamed of them, they could not by force of will make themselves feel attracted to people of the opposite sex.

David's sexual history and fantasy life seem clearly heterosexual. During his teens and twenties, he had several fantasized relations with young women, particularly a young Mexican woman, the daughter of a family with whom we stayed in Cuernavaca. Over the course of several years, David wrote long ardent letters in Spanish to this young woman, which she occasionally reciprocated. Later he imagined some attraction to other young women whom he met, but not of the same duration.

David has had at least two heterosexual experiences that we know about. While visiting friends in Washington before leaving for Cambridge, England, in 1976, a young woman took him to bed after a party. David found this experience gratifying and affirmative; that is, unlike the experience with the gay older man, there was no trace of shame or guilt about this experience. David also had a sexual experience with a female friend while in Cambridge. He may have had other such sexual experiences, but has not told us about them. For a while he became interested in "girly magazines," which he pored over, although he has not done so recently.

What mainly characterizes David's sexuality is its immaturity. Sexually, David seems frozen in mid-adolescence, having never moved on to an actual sexual relationship as a friendship nor bonding for even the shortest time with a female or male. During a recent hospitalization, a staff member complained to us that David masturbated. This had never been mentioned to us before, but it may have been going on for some time. We don't necessarily see masturbation as "bad," but rather an expression of someone who feels sexual urges but is unable to express them with another human being.

Since his crisis months at school in England, David has not been able to make deep friendships of any kind, male or female, although he occasionally seems to have positive associations. His vehement homophobia comes out when there seems to be any hint of a man coming on to him, and this doubtless reflects his negative experience as a teen. But one should not assume that this reflects a repression of homosexual attraction. The evidence of his fantasy life and limited sexual experience suggests an immature, inhibited, but heterosexual orientation. One odd wrinkle in this question of David's sexual and personal maturity occurred in early 2005 (some ten years after leaving Hawaii) when David, out of the blue, claimed to have a daughter in Hawaii. Later, he even expanded this to claim two daughters. When we inquired about the mother, he said she was a beautiful girl at Kahumana with whom he had had a relationship. This was a surprise to us, and we are inclined to dismiss it as a fantasy. Such a thing might be possible, of course, but since the Kahumana community is fairly tight knit, we assume that if David had had such children, someone would have informed us.

Why David would suddenly claim this paternity after such a long period is mysterious. Perhaps it is a way of competing with his younger sister who is married with two children. Recently he asked me somewhat wistfully whether I thought he had children or not. I said I didn't know, but I thought if he did someone from Hawaii would have told us. Somehow thinking that he has children seems comforting to David, but, notably, he seems to have no thought whatsoever that having children might entail some responsibility on his part.

David's Hawaiian Experience

After leaving Kahumana David remained in Hawaii for another six years. He was assigned a social worker who established a relationship with David and stayed with him as long as he was a resident of Hawaii and enrolled in the state health care system. David's social worker got him on Supplemental Security Income (SSI) for the first time in his life and connected him with a clinic where he received an expensive experimental drug called Clozaril, which seemed to make him function much better. Hawaii's system for assigning social workers was clearly superior to what we would have experienced in Illinois and California, and we were relieved to have a person we could contact to find out what was happening with David.

The Hawaiian health care system consists of three interconnected parts: mental wards of hospitals, out-patient clinics, and small board-and-care homes run by families who provide housing for four to six patients in units added to their own homes. During his years in Hawaii, David experienced all of these facilities, bouncing in and out of hospitals eight times over six years, regularly visiting the clinic that monitored his medications and did blood tests, and living in four family care homes. No care home lasted more than two years. Always some incident—fighting with another resident or acting inappropriately, like running outside naked—would land David in a hospital ward and then there would be another placement.

David went on long walks around the island, sometimes having the experience of visioning a "paradise" where he could "live forever." Once he told us that he had discovered the Garden of Eden, but he knew he couldn't stay. A free bus system that circulated the island facilitated his travels. Generally, he seemed to get back to his care home by the end of the day.

In 1995 David's situation deteriorated. He became paranoid about riding in cars on freeways and on more than one occasion, he opened the car door and jumped out. For a while he was homeless, sleeping in the backyard of a clinic, and he spent a few days at a drop-in shelter in Honolulu. Finally, David's social worker arranged for David to return to

Illinois. In fall 1995 David flew into the Chicago airport. Since we were out of town at the time, his younger sister met him and drove him to his new home at the La Grange YMCA, where David could participate regularly in a nearby mental health program.

Chicago Again: 1995–2002

The next seven years were a constant cycle of hopes and failures. David resided in four board-and-care facilities, most fairly large, dingy, urine-smelling, multifloor urban hotels with two to four patients to a room. None of these facilities provided any real activities, though they made a pretense of doing so. David had stays at four or five hospitals, where his condition was briefly stabilized through medication. He also stayed in three nursing home facilities, where people with mental illness and others with physical handicaps lived alongside elderly residents. This practice, which is common in Chicago, seemed very dubious to us, but David actually seemed comfortable in these mixed facilities and got along better there than in facilities solely for those with mental illness. One reason for this is that the nursing homes were cheerful and clean and generally had ample trained staff.

For a time David lived in a board-and-care facility in the Near North Side of Chicago, close to a park and the zoo. This very pleasant neighborhood with its many restaurants and theaters is popular among young professionals. But most important for us, it was only a few blocks from Thresholds, which is reputed to be the best mental health program in Chicago and in the United States in general. Fifteen years earlier David had participated in this program for a few months before dropping out. We had high hopes that it might work out this time, but it was a complete bust. David would walk to Thresholds, but not go in. After hanging around outside for a while, he would return to his room. David lacked the self-confidence to walk in by himself and get involved in the activities, and there wasn't anyone at the door to help him do so.

Herman and I followed David through these various changes of address, visiting him, checking on his clothes, and tending to his general well-being. When possible, we took him on excursions. Sometimes we drove him to Evanston to spend the afternoon in our home, where he might help his father with some chore, such as gardening, and have a meal.

David Develops the "Flips"

David developed a self-destructive behavior that we came to call "the flips" because he would literally flip over benches and tables or somersault down stairs. Once in a bookstore with his father, he "flipped" from a second-floor balcony to a book table on the first floor. It became difficult to take him to restaurants, because he would suddenly flip backward in his chair. I began to anticipate from David's silence and the concentrated look on his face when this might happen. I would try to rush him outdoors, thinking that on grass he wasn't as likely to break something or to injure himself. Nonetheless, David's flipping behavior resulted in several injuries. He broke a foot when he flipped over the stair railing on the second floor of our house. At one board-and-care home, he flipped down the stairs on several occasions, one time breaking an arm. But the most disastrous flip was on the stairs in another care home where David broke an arm *and* shattered his ankle, which resulted in a prolonged hospital stay and the near amputation of his foot. For several months David had to wear a device on his leg with metal pins extending into his leg bone. The ankle healed eventually, but it is permanently deformed, as is his foot.

What was the reason for David's "flipping" behavior? Knowing that he might be injured, why did he persist in throwing his body around so violently? I have two theories. One is that David's flipping is a kind of self-induced "shock therapy." When the voices and inner tensions become unbearable, violent motion somehow brings relief. The other theory, which doesn't exclude the first, is that flipping is a way of getting out of an unpleasant place. David's headlong flip down the stairs at Winston Manor resulted in a broken arm, and similar behavior at The Wilson cost him an arm and an ankle, but the net result was that he was removed, at least temporarily, from those facilities and placed in a more pleasant hospital. Was this David's intent? He never suggests so. Rather, he claims to aspire to some kind of "accomplishment"—namely that he should be able to fly through the air, perform a perfect flip, and land lightly on his feet.

Family Commitments and Restrictions

Over the many years of David's struggle with mental illness, Herman and I have gradually developed what I would call a combination of "grace" and "limits" with respect to our relationship with our son. By grace I mean that we want to remain permanently committed to David no matter what he does, no matter how incapable he becomes of forging a more positive path through life. This, of course, is a problematic commitment since we are not getting any younger and David shows no signs of becoming independent. It is also evident that despite the services the state provides for David, the responsibility for truly caring for him ultimately falls to his family. As long as David and we are alive, Herman and I will be there for him. However, this does not mean that we don't have deep ambivalences about the effects David has on our lives.

A few months after the onset of David's schizophrenia, Herman and I determined that we were not going to let David's illness destroy our life or to so absorb our energies that we would have no life of our own. An incident took place after David's return from England that cemented this conviction for me. David had been living with us for six very intense months, during which we had made the rounds of therapists and hospitals with our son and had been subjected to his outbursts of violence. Finally I decided it was time to reclaim some space in my life that wasn't given over to David. I decided to have an open house and invite my faculty colleagues to see our new home.

David reacted to this announcement with surprise, saying, "No, we can't have these kind of social events anymore." With some shock I realized that David had given up any expectation that he could develop his own life in the outside world. He wanted only to withdraw into our home, pull its four walls around him to shield him from the world, and depend on us to guard his refuge. I understood then that not only must we have an open house, we had to continue to have a social life, regardless of whether or not David is able to "have a life." What this has come to mean in practice is that David cannot live with us nor can he come and go freely from our home. We maintain contact and are committed to our relationship with David, but the time he spends with us and in our home is limited to afternoon and early-evening visits of four to six hours once, twice, and sometimes three times a week, depending on his proximity.

David's sisters have their own approaches to understanding and relating to their brother. Both are saddened by his sickness, but they are also clear about their need to live their own lives, which include demanding jobs and, for our youngest daughter, two growing children. David's older sister has a deeper ambivalence toward him. For a while, Becky had a hard time believing that her brother was really mentally ill and thought he was simply "pretending" in order to escape responsibility for his life. She is critical of medication and sees it as primarily sedating him, rather than helping him. She is annoyed by David's occasional expression of a provocative and sometimes salacious fantasy life. She herself has some physical health problems, and she doesn't feel she can allow him to threaten the fragile balance by which she maintains her life. As the sister closest to him in age and in childhood experiences, Becky particularly finds David's decline distressing, but she feels that she cannot help him and also cannot be vulnerable to him.

David's younger sister is less emotionally conflicted by his situation. But David's illness concerns her because she worries whether one of her own children might be vulnerable to mental illness. Mimi often arranged to visit with David when he lived in Chicago and would sometimes take him to a movie or out to eat. David had a hard time relating appropriately to Mimi's children when they were small and did things like swing his leg over their heads. Mimi's older son, then about four or five, sensed this as strange behavior and exhibited wariness toward Uncle David. Now that David is in California and Mimi lives with her family in Chicago, she can no longer visit him regularly, but on Christmas trips to our home she makes a point of seeing him at least once.

For both Becky and Mimi, the question of who will take responsibility for David and how to do so when we are no longer here remains moot. Clearly, neither of them feels able to step into the role that Herman and I are presently playing. When I discussed this book with my youngest daughter, she recalled an incident that happened almost thirty years ago when all five Ruethers were participating in family therapy. At one point Herman, David, and I went out of the room. The therapist then turned to Becky and Mimi, and said to them pointedly, "Someday this will be your responsibility."

California: 2002 to the Present

Herman and I moved to California in mid-July 2002, and David, who at the time was in fairly good shape physically and mentally, went with us. He was very excited about the move and had asked me if the place where he was to stay had a swimming pool. I said, "No," but the place where we were going to live had one, which he could use.

The flight to California went very well. David was cheerful and enjoyed the food and the in-flight movie. The next morning we took him to his new residence, which turned out to be a cluster of one-story cottages around a patio, just off a busy main street. I had arranged to pay extra so he could have his own room, but from the moment we stepped into the facility, it was evident that David was disappointed. Clearly, his new residence, with the usual array of psychiatric patients, clustered in small groups in chairs on the patio, quietly talking to each other, did not meet with his rosy vision of life in California.

Arranging Supplemental Security Income (SSI) payments for David's medications proved difficult. We spent several days at the Social Security office in Pomona arranging for David's transfer to Cal-Med. I had to pay out of pocket for his first month of medications, which cost more than $1,000. Finally things were worked out for his state support.

During our first month in California we saw David almost every day. He accompanied us on endless trips to purchase furniture and other items for our new house. We bought David a desk and a bookcase for his new room and investigated getting a typewriter, which he wanted for his writing. But the constant contact would of necessity lessen as September approached, because I would begin teaching in Berkeley and would come home only every third weekend. Herman could continue to see David, but not as frequently.

But before September arrived it was evident that David was not comfortable at his new residence in Claremont. He hid himself away in his room and imagined that the residents were all talking about him. I found him on one occasion standing in a corner behind the door to his room. David was also hostile to the doctor and refused to talk with him. This amazed the doctor, a very pleasant and hearty gentleman, who was accustomed to a having good relations with patients.

Soon we got reports that David was hitting people. After assaulting a staff member, he was expelled from the facility. The owner very kindly contacted another facility in South El Monte, about a half hour away, that agreed to take David. We scooped him up with his meager belongings and drove him to the new residence, lodged in a former Catholic convent.

South El Monte is primarily a Hispanic community of one-story homes owned by working-class people who take great care of their residences and gardens. The board-and-care facility there consisted of a two-story residence, which served as an office for the director and housing for some staff, with a cluster of cottages behind. Each cottage had a bathroom, a living room, and several bedrooms, with one or two beds in each. Another small building housed a dining room and a second room that was purportedly for activities, though these never seemed to actually happen.

South El Monte is typical of many facilities in the United States for people with mental illness; Hispanics and Asians, mostly immigrants without any special job training, serve as caretakers. Doubtless this reflects the low pay available for such work. At South El Monte the director, who was Sikh, ran the facility almost single handedly, managing financially by having a minimum of paid staff and sometimes using his teenage son as a helper. I doubt that the director or either of the facility's two staff persons had degrees in mental health, but they were kind and intelligent. The director viewed the patients as people who shouldn't be expected to be rational. Occasionally he would yell at patients and strong-arm them into compliance, but overall the staff was remarkably calm, seeking to keep a minimal order. The agenda for such facilities is focused on maintaining the status quo, rather than encouraging people to develop. Most psychiatric patients at such facilities seem content with a passive life of eating, sleeping, and watching TV. David was not content. The director arranged for David to go to a "program," which seemed to us to consist of little more than acquiring treats, exercising (music and dancing), watching television or movies, and art activities. There was no emphasis on developing skills or preparing for employment. David lasted at South El Monte for two years and eight months, thanks largely to the extraordinary forbearance of the director.

David's Mood Swings and Wanderings

During his time at South El Monte David's mood went in cycles. At times he was affable and capable of sustaining some activities with us. We took him to numerous parks in the area for walking and swimming. A nearby miniature golf course also provided several afternoons of recreation. We got him a bicycle, and he enjoyed riding it around the fairly quiet and safe streets of residential South El Monte.

At times we drove David back to our home at Pilgrim Place to swim, to walk in the Claremont Botanic Garden, and to eat a meal at our house. We visited several museums in the Los Angeles and Pasadena area, including the Huntington Gardens, which David liked very much. At the Huntington, we usually did not visit the museum but took the garden walk instead, as David did not seem able to sustain the tension of looking at the pictures with other groups of people. For a while movies became a regular activity.

But at other times we would arrive with plans for an "outing" only to be received with hostility—sometimes a stream of vituperation or simply a moodiness—that made it clear that David was not able to sustain activities with us. In those cases we either left immediately or, if we had started out on an excursion, turned the car around and took him back to his board-and-care home.

It was also at this time that David began what would become periodic marathon walking sprees. When life seemed to become intolerable for him at his residence, he would take off for a long walk, either to our home in Claremont or to his sister's apartment in Redondo Beach. Our Claremont home is about twenty miles away from South El Monte, linked by a busy freeway and with no very direct local roads. Although we tried to instruct him on how to take buses, David mainly would walk this distance over a day or a day and a half, sleeping along the way. He would arrive footsore but ebullient at his achievement. We would give him a bath, wash his clothes, take him for a swim if he was up for it, and then have a meal at our house, after which we would return him to his residence. He was always willing to return, since we had made clear that staying with us more permanently was not an option. He did so, not happily so much as resigned to his fate.

More troubling were his long walks to Redondo Beach, a trip of some forty miles through major Los Angeles urban streets. To our surprise, no one ever robbed or hurt him, and he met several people who helped him, even though the streets he traversed passed through neighborhoods considered dangerous. When he had been in better shape we took David for a couple of outings to his sister's apartment and for a swim at the beach, so he had some idea of where her apartment was, although his ability to walk there from South El Monte was something we had never imagined. His arrival was extremely unwelcome to his sister, who was horrified that he might turn up at her house and want to stay. Becky was very busy managing her own life and demanding job. She clearly did not want to have her brother imposing himself on her space. She talked of moving away to another area where he would not know where she was.

The first time David walked to her apartment, Becky drove him back to South El Monte. The second time he showed up, she refused him entrance to her apartment. He hung around on the beach and was picked up by the police while rifling through a Dumpster for food. Taken to a public hospital, and then to a psychiatric hospital, he was eventually returned to the board-and-care home in South El Monte. We told him that he could come to our house if he felt he had to, preferably by bus, and we would receive him briefly, but under no circumstances was he to go to his sister's.

Life Moves On

David's attitude toward his two sisters is ambivalent, oscillating between playful, slightly hostile references and wonderment that they have responsible jobs. He seems to have a hard time imagining that his sisters have moved on since they were all teenagers. Both finished college and earned graduate degrees, while David's life has only gone downhill since he was seventeen. Becky is a computer animator at a leading Los Angeles company and Mimi is a lawyer for the city of Chicago. Once or twice David has asked, "Is Mimi really a lawyer?" What Becky does for a living escaped him altogether until we took him to a movie she had worked on and he saw her name in the credits.

David also has a hard time imagining what we do with our days, and has sometimes asked, "What do you do all day?" I reply that we garden, swim, and read books, feeling I should not overwhelm him with the actual complexity of our lives, which stand in such stark contrast to his pathetically diminished existence.

David's Hospitalizations

In the thirty-two months that he lived at South El Monte, David was hospitalized at least six times, usually at a small facility solely for persons with mental illness in the Hawthorne area of Los Angeles. The doctors never contacted us when David was hospitalized, and our calls to them were never returned, even though we made the long trek of more than an hour to see him at least once a week. Generally, these hospitalizations lasted two weeks, during which time medications were used to "stabilize" David so he could be released and return to his residence. The doctors, who were overworked and changed continually, never told us what medications David was on, and we found it difficult to discover what medications the hospital had prescribed for him. Other than sending a list of prescribed medications to David's board-and-care home, the doctors didn't follow up on David after releasing him from the hospital, nor did the social workers who were responsible for arranging placements for David upon leaving the hospital.

During David's hospitalizations we found the social workers we dealt with to be somewhat more responsive than the doctors. Even then, however, we always had to initiate contact, and it was up to us to keep the lines of communication open. The typical hospital program was passive and offered little to engage David. Nonetheless, he attended group sessions during which things such as hygiene and grooming were addressed; nothing was discussed of future education or employment. There was little opportunity for exercise, other than dancing and occasionally basketball on the hospital patio. Patients were not expected to perform chores, not even caring for one's own property or self. Cigarettes were handed out freely and seemed to be a means of sedating patients. David, who had been proud that he had been able to free himself from cigarette smoking five years earlier in Hawaii, was gradually induced to take up smoking again.

David was hospitalized several times for fights with another male resident, who himself seemed to be as much or more the aggressor. The director seemed not to blame David too much for these incidents and accepted him back after the usual two weeks' stay in the hospital. Then David began to act out physically in ways that caused injury to himself, tumbling over benches and fences, and his increasing use of cigarettes (which were handed out daily by the director) began to take a toll on David's room. We continually counseled David not to smoke in his room, which was forbidden, but his compliance with this rule was minimal.

In the spring of 2005 David exploded in his room, breaking furniture and smashing his guitar. He was sent to the hospital with a clear indication from the director that he would not be accepted back. After several weeks back at the hospital, David was placed in another facility in the heart of Koreatown in Los Angeles.

This facility was a two-story former rooming house. David shared a second-floor room with a roommate whom he seemed to like at first, saying he was "the best roommate I have ever had." Having a roommate he liked forced David to socialize a bit, rather than hiding in his room. The director seemed very affable, and at first he lauded David as a fine resident. But there was something about the man that did not ring true to me. He seemed to be a glad-hander who talked a good line about how well organized his facility was, but I suspected that the reality was quite different from the rhetoric.

We visited David several times in his new residence and took him to nearby Griffith Park for picnics and to the zoo. But David was severely plagued by voices and could hardly sustain a conversation or even a visit with us for more than an hour or two. One late afternoon David disappeared, apparently telling people he was going to his parents' house. For five days he walked around Los Angeles with little sense of the geography, initially heading west toward LAX and then turning around and walking east. He ended up at Echo Park, a few miles from his board-and-care home, near downtown Los Angeles. A kindly stranger undertook to call us and we in turn arranged for David to return to his residence.

At that point the director and staff seemed perfectly happy to accept him back. But soon David's behavior deteriorated. His feeling of alienation from the other residents kept him from attending meals, which meant that it was also likely he wasn't getting his medications. Neither the director nor the staff seemed to notice this behavior, and it was some time before we became aware of it. We wonder if they would have allowed David simply to starve to death.

One day David exploded, throwing his desk and bookcase out the window of his room. They damaged a car in the parking lot below, for which we had to pay. The director of the care facility called the police, who took David to a public hospital. As in such situations previously, we had great difficulty getting information as to his whereabouts. At first we were told that the public hospital had discharged him, and under the impression that he was wandering about, we reported him as a missing person. We learned afterward that David had been transferred to White Memorial Hospital in Boyle Heights, an area just south and west of downtown Los Angeles. After great difficulty and much persistence, we managed to be in contact with someone who acknowledged that David was in the hospital. We were never given the name of a social worker, though one would think such information would be readily provided to family members who were obviously concerned about the patient and interested in his well-being.

We visited David at White Memorial and were struck by his extreme nervousness. The voices were plaguing him severely. He was happy, however, that he had been interviewed and accepted in another board-and-care home. We planned to visit David again the following week, but were told that he had been discharged. We were amazed that no one had thought to contact us to inform us of David's release. It was as if we didn't even exist. There wasn't a social worker available on the weekend, and no one else could tell us where he was. Consequently, it was the following Monday before we were finally able to speak to a social worker and learn that David had been discharged the previous Thursday or Friday; she was not sure which. She told us that David had been offered transportation to the new care home, but he said he would get there on his own. He was left to do so, which astonished us, since David didn't know where this care home was located nor did he have the means to get there on his own.

David wandered for five days without money, food, or water. We tried to file a missing-person report, but got continual runarounds from the Los Angeles Police Department. Finally, the Claremont police agreed to register a missing-person report. On Wednesday afternoon David showed up at his former board-and-care home, hungry and asking for food. The director was extremely averse to allowing David to stay, but some staff women fed him and allowed him to spend the night. However, because David was no longer a resident, we were faced with trying to get him placed in a hospital ourselves.

We drove to David's former care facility and found him sitting on a bench outside the residence. His story was different from the one we had been told by White Memorial. According to David the hospital had told him there would be transportation to his new board-and-care home. For a time he had stood outside the hospital with a girl who was also waiting for transportation. Eventually, she was taken away in a cab, but he was told to wait. After waiting and waiting for transportation to arrive, he had started to walk. David claimed that he walked to Commonwealth Avenue, where he met some people who gave him money and food. He stayed with them for four days and then decided to walk back to his former residence. David said that he was aware that he would not be taken in, but he didn't know where else to go.

David was tanned but thin when we found him, having lost sixty pounds over the previous few weeks. He actually looked remarkably well and seemed quite cheerful. As instructed by the Los Angeles hospital, we drove him to an emergency facility in Bellflower, which did the intake clearance and then sent him on to a hospital.

After some weeks in the hospital, it became time for David to be released. The social worker assigned to David seemed particularly inept, so the work of finding a new place for David fell to us. Herman and I were determined that David would go to a board-and-care home more convenient for us. We searched a list of such places near our home and got positive responses from several. We chose a medium-size place in South Pomona within a fifteen-minute drive of our home. The hospital arranged for David's transfer. The social worker, who had done nothing to assist us with David's new placement, took credit for having "found" David a place.

This board-and-care facility was located in a poorer, mostly Hispanic neighborhood of apartments and small single-family homes. It looked like it might have been a motel at one time. David suggested as much, but he also claimed it had been a prisoner-of-war concentration camp. The facility was made up of several rows of buildings. Each building had three units comprising four rooms, with two beds per room, and a bathroom. At one time there may have been a swimming pool in a small side yard, but when David lived there, the only recreation available was a basketball hoop. Allegedly, basic math and reading classes were offered, and some residents gathered to play games, like Bingo. David had no interest in the games or classes apart from a cooking class that afforded him the opportunity to acquire a soda from the kitchen refrigerator. The food served at meals was heavy on starches. Lunch regularly consisted of baloney sandwiches or Ramen noodles, but something fancier, like tacos, was served several times a week. Cake and ice cream appeared for special holidays and birthdays.

The people in charge—a man and two women—were Filipino and were part of a network that included another such institution in a nearby city. The man had some medical training, and the person who dispensed medications was fairly responsible about doing so. They figured out quickly that we could be an asset in helping control David's behavior, so they called to talk with us whenever there was an issue with David, which we appreciated. They regularly made arrangements for the weekly blood tests that David needed because he was on Clozaril, and they also arranged for him to get to dental appointments.

The atmosphere at the residence was very permissive. The patients, about a third female and two-thirds male, sometimes walked around barefoot or in socks. While generally adequately clothed, they often dressed oddly and were scruffy in appearance. Many passed the time sitting outside talking; others spent hours rocking back and forth or lying on the ground muttering, cursing, or shouting. Patients were free to walk in and out of the facility at will, but the staff seemed able to keep track of them, and they were aware if anyone disappeared for more than a day.

Increased Physical Ailments

David's physical health while at the Pomona board-and-care proved to be a roller coaster of ups and downs. Two months after moving in, he took a "flip" and broke his hip. He was sent to a hospital for surgery and then transferred to a nursing home, which provided some minimal rehabilitation. David found this place intolerably restrictive, however, and soon made himself unacceptable.

Soon after returning to the Pomona home, David developed a severe infection of a bursitis on the elbow that he had injured while living in Illinois. Every time David was hospitalized, we had appealed to the doctors and staff to look at the sack of fluid on his elbow. They always promised to do so, but never did. In time we realized that mental illness facilities do not regard patients' physical problems as their responsibility. Likewise, medical hospitals ignore physical problems other than those for which the patient is admitted. Consequently, no one paid attention to the bursitis on David's elbow and it became seriously infected.

A staff person at David's board-and-care home arranged for him to go to Los Angeles Metropolitan Hospital, where doctors administered antibiotics and then did surgery on his elbow. David was sent back to Pomona, but the elbow was still dripping pus so he was sent to a different hospital. They, too, administered antibiotics, but unable to cope with David's mental issues, they sent him on to another medical center in Culver City that has units for both physical and mental health. After several rocky weeks in the regular medical unit, David was sent up to the fifth-floor psych unit, where both his psychological and physical problems were attended to.

Following more intensive surgery, David was sent to a nursing facility in Pasadena for rehabilitation. He was there for several months as his elbow healed. We visited him about twice a week and found the facility clean and pleasant enough for people who need permanent nursing care, which David doesn't. It was a standard institution of this type with perhaps 200 patients, usually two to a room. The population was a combination of elderly and chronically ill paitients, along with a few recovering patients who could expect to leave. I suspect that many were on psychotropic medications, although I don't have data on that. Clearly, David was given such medications, along with medical drugs, such as antibiotics. He had an IV in his hand all the time he was there.

Other than reading or watching television, patients had few activities to choose from. There was an organized program that consisted mostly of games conducted by a recreation specialist. David found them boring and geared to the elderly; he never participated. There were two or three exercise machines for physical rehabilitation, which David liked using and thought of as serious activity. The highlight of the day was the cigarette break, which took place about every two hours on a regular schedule from after breakfast through early evening. For David it was a not-to-be-missed event, and sometimes we would have to hurry back from an outdoor excursion so he could attend the cigarette break. Nursing homes, mental hospitals, and board-and-care homes seem not to have heard that cigarettes are bad for one's health. All distribute them and organize opportunities for patients to smoke.

In spring 2006, when his elbow was finally pronounced healed, David returned to Pomona.

Growing Older and "Aging Out"

David's behavior mellowed after returning to Pomona. We now saw little evidence of the angry man who had in the past wreaked havoc on our home and other property and lashed out at us and at others. David is still plagued with multiple "voices" that demean him, and he is given to a variety of fantasies and obsessions. He believes, for example, that his little finger is broken and that a tooth pulled by a dentist in 2002 has deeply impaired his psycho-bodily wholeness. He is also obsessed with the idea that people steal his notebooks and publish his writings.

Daniel's mellowing may be an expression of "aging out," which is a pattern some mental health experts have identified in which people with schizophrenia seem to lose some of the most virulent symptoms of the disease as they approach their fifties. I don't see aging out as evidence that David's medication is finally working but that it's likely he now requires less medication, although it is not evident that he can be weaned from it altogether.

Although David was getting along reasonably well at the Pomona board-and-care, he constantly hoped to find a more satisfactory place to live. Unquestionably, it is a marginal place. The neighborhood is dangerous and the clientele is scruffy. David claimed that several of the female patients were involved in prostitution; in fact, on two occasions we saw women being dropped off at the facility in a manner that seemed odd. The facility also had a reputation for drug dealing; we did observe communication across a particular fence that seemed suspicious to us. David thought that drug dealing was happening, though, thankfully, he wasn't interested in taking part in it.

Patients also engaged in a lively trade in cheaply acquired goods including televisions, refrigerators, coffee makers, and other appliances. David acquired several such items for very little money, though some no longer worked. Patients also picked up bags of food from a nearby food bank to sell to other patients. David purchased food in this manner, but he also got food directly from the food bank. Stealing was rife among patients. David regularly lost money or personal items, although it is hard to sort out what was actually taken and what he misplaced and claimed someone stole. Still, David's tales of people coming into his room and stealing things could not be attributed only to fantasies born of paranoia. A heater was stolen and later returned, but food, money, and clothes constantly disappeared. David was harassed regularly by a resident who lived with his girlfriend in a neighboring unit. (Sexual coupling seems to be allowed.) David believed the man stole his wallet and other items. Generally, the staff did little to counteract such stealing, choosing instead to let the patients work it out between themselves, but they did transfer David to a different unit.

In March 2009, through the intervention of his social worker, David moved into a new place in La Verne, California, which is even closer to our home. This was the first time that David moved from a board-and-care home voluntarily, instead of being thrown out for bad behavior. In fact, the managers at the Pomona facility expressed regret that he was leaving and assured David that he would be welcome to return if he wanted to.

David's new residence is clean and pleasant and in a much better neighborhood, but it has the atmosphere of a nursing home and most of the residents are in wheelchairs. Previously, David had vehemently rejected this option, but then he accepted it. He seems content there for the moment, but it too is unsatisfactory as a place where he can have any real community or outreach to activities.

David continues to be very passive. He depends largely on us for activities and relationship, and his dependency and lack of self-initiative causes us concern. It is hard to imagine what will happen to him as we get older and more infirm, and die, which is likely to happen in the next ten to twenty years, since Herman was born in 1930 and I in 1936. David seems to have no concept of how to survive without us.

We are constantly casting around for new options for him for work, housing, education, and social life. In order to encourage David to be active and to enlarge his social circle, we try to involve him in a variety of activities on his thrice-weekly visits with us. Some Tuesdays we volunteer at the Beta Center, a food pantry where David and I organize donated food to be given to the clients. On Fridays we may take part in the peace demonstration to protest the wars in Iraq and Afghanistan and the threats of war against Iran. The demonstration is organized by some members of the Pilgrim Place community where we live. At David's request, we began attending the youth Mass at Our Lady of Assumption Parish a half block from our home in Claremont. He seemed to enjoy the popular music and youth participation, but he has since grown tired of its enthusiastic style. I also save up my errands, from picking up or dropping off papers at school to shopping for food and household items, and do these with David. He enjoys doing these activities with me and is helpful in carrying loads and suggesting ideas for meals. Thus I combine doing things I have to do with being with him and getting him to help me.

In November 2008 David began pushing the limits of the agreed-on times for visits to our home. He would show up unexpectedly, having walked the entire way. On several occasions this caused serious inconvenience, particularly when he arrived while I was teaching a class that meets weekly in our home. Since David had difficulty returning to his residence by bus, we generally had to drive him back, which was a further inconvenience. We became very insistent that David respect the schedule for visits to our home, even while conceding that his unexpected arrivals are likely to continue. We have since found a better way of dealing with this issue. Shortly after David moved to his current residence, we helped him tune up his bike and get a bike lock installed. A few days later David showed up at our house on his bike, looking very pleased with himself after successfully negotiating three miles of busy streets. Herman congratulated him on his accomplishment, gave him a meal, and then sent him off to return to his residence, which he did willingly.

Sometimes during his visits to our home, I help David enter his writings on the computer. This task gives him great satisfaction. Some of what David has written, in both English and Spanish, was composed in pencil during his stays at the psychiatric hospital in Hawthorne, California. David shares his reflections on questionable aspects of the mental health system. He also reflects on cultural hypocrisies, writing in a stream-of-consciousness style that includes flashes of insight and wit. David's writings reveal a surprisingly sophisticated vocabulary. He spells well but occasionally makes up words.

One day after we finished entering some of his work on the computer, David shared his worries that at some time in the future he might have to "live outdoors."

"Do you mean, being homeless?" I asked.

"Yes," he replied. David then went on to say that he worried about what would happen to him when we died. "Maybe we could arrange a liturgy where I would die also," he suggested.

I replied that I hoped to find him better housing in a community where he could be happy without us.

Later that day, while sitting at the dining room table, David commented, "I still have hope that my life can be interesting."

2 Symptoms of What?

Official Symptoms and David's Experiences

The official system of diagnosis of mental illness is defined by the guidelines of the American Psychiatric Association in the *DSM* or *Diagnostic and Statistical Manual of Mental Disorders.* This manual has grown considerably since it was first published in 1952. At that time a bare two pages were devoted to schizophrenia in a slim pamphlet of 137 pages. Schizophrenia was defined in this way:

> This term is synonymous with the formerly used term dementia praecox. It represents a group of psychotic reactions characterized by fundamental disturbances in reality relationships and concept formations, with affective, behavioral and intellectual disturbances in varying degrees and mixtures. The disorders are marked by strong tendencies to retreat from reality, by emotional disharmony, unpredictable disturbances in stream of thought, regressive behavior and in some a tendency to "deterioration."[1]

Schizophrenia was divided into several types: "simple type," characterized by withdrawal from reality, but without hallucinations; "hebephrenic type," silliness, unpredictable giggling, delusions, hallucinations, and regressive behavior; "catatonic type," characterized by stupor and mutism or excessive motor activity; and "paranoid type," characterized by delusions of persecution, grandiose ideas, and ideas of reference. Also described are acute and chronic undifferentiated types where these symptoms are mixed and the schizo-affective type where schizophrenic and bipolar symptoms are mixed.

The description of schizophrenia in the 2000 edition of the *DSM* (*Diagnostic and Statistical Manual of Mental Disorders*, 4th edition, Transition) has grown considerably over the years. It now is twenty-six pages out of a total manual of 943 pages. The section on schizophrenia details a number of issues, such as genetic factors and brain scan images differentiating the brains of schizophrenics from "normal" brains. These are acknowledged to be inconclusive, and such evidence as there is may be due to the use of neuroleptic drugs, rather than the disease.

A large number of motor symptoms, such as tardive dyskinesia, neuroleptic-induced parkinsonism, neuroleptic-induced acute akathisia, neuroleptic-induced acute dystonia, neuroleptic malignant syndromes (various kinds of chronic twitches and shakes)[3] are identified as caused by the neuroleptic medication. Also the symptoms of affective flattening, passivity, and loss of volition may also be side effects of medication or the result of "chronic environmental under-stimulation."[4] The manual does not identify what this might be, but it sounds like the effect of being shut up in a repressive environment, like the back ward of a mental hospital or confined to a nursing home or a dreary board-and-care home.

The *DSM-IV-TR*, like its predecessors, lists a number of symptoms that together define what is called schizophrenia. The term itself is misleading, since it literally means "split-mind." However, schizophrenia as defined in current medical usage does not mean "split personality," but a concatenation of symptoms of "impaired perception of reality." Swiss psychiatrist Eugen Bleuler coined the term in 1908 to describe what he saw as a separation of function between personality, thinking, memory, and perception.[5] There is no agreed-on physical cause of schizophrenia in the sense of biological tests that can confirm its presence. Thus, diagnosis is based on the presence of various symptoms that are self-reported or reported by others, such as family members, and/or observed by clinicians.

The current *DSM* differentiates symptoms into two categories. These are positive symptoms and negative symptoms. The positive symptoms include delusions, auditory hallucinations, and thought disorder. The negative or deficit symptoms are the loss or absence of "normal" functions, such as flat or blunted affect, poverty of speech, and lack of motivation and energy.

> The positive symptoms appear to reflect an excess or distortion of normal functions, whereas the negative symptoms appear to reflect a diminution or loss of normal functions. The positive symptoms include distortions of thought content (delusions), perception (hallucinations), language and thought process (disorganized speech), and self-monitoring of behavior (grossly disorganized or catatonic behavior). These positive symptoms may comprise two distinct dimensions, which may in turn be related to different underlying neural mechanisms and clinical correlates. The "psychotic dimension" includes delusions and hallucinations, whereas the "disorganization dimension" includes disorganized speech and behavior. Negative symptoms include restrictions on the range and intensity of emotional expression (affective flattening), in the fluency and productivity of thought and speech (alogia) and in the initiation of goal-directed behavior (avolition).[6]

Like the earlier *DSM*, *DSM-IV-TR* divides schizophrenia into subtypes: paranoid type, disorganized type (the new name for hebephrenic), catatonic type, undifferentiated type, and residual type. There are now separate categories for schizophreniform disorder and schizoaffective disorder. I will focus on the "paranoid type," which is David's diagnosis. This is seen as present when the person hears voices that are threatening, believes that people are watching or following him or her, experiences ideas as being inserted into one's mind by hostile others, or believes that others can read one's mind or that one's ideas are being broadcast to others. Ideas of reference are common; that is, believing that events happening around one, such as someone coughing on the other side of the street and a plane going overhead at the same time, refer to some planned conspiracy against oneself. It is recognized that not all these symptoms are present in everyone defined as a schizophrenic and those that are present appear in very individualistic ways in each person.

In this chapter I will discuss some number of the symptoms that David has experienced over the years (these have changed from his early onset in the late 1970s to recent experiences in 2006–2009) and ask to what extent these experiences can be proven to be symptoms of "illness" or "disease," as distinct from variants of common human experiences, learned behavior, or effects of medication.

Hearing Voices: What Do They Mean?

The psychiatric system takes the hearing of "voices" as prime evidence of the presence of that mental illness they call schizophrenia. They interpret it to be an expression of some malfunction of the brain, currently blamed on the neurotransmitters.

David has heard "voices" for more than twenty-eight years, beginning in about 1980. These voices appear to be multiple, both male and female. In his earlier years of hearing voices, David seemed to have a lot of interaction with television and radio, experiencing people in the media as if they were referring to him (ideas of reference). Lately he seems much less involved in hearing media personalities, like news commentator Connie Chung, but certain rock stars are still very important to him and he often imagines some relation to David Bowie. In April 2008 David's wallet was stolen from the board-and-care home where he was living at the time. He presumed that a resident in an adjacent room with whom he had had difficulties had taken it. This seemed a likely suspicion, not paranoia, but in discussing it, he suddenly said that he "heard" that David Bowie had taken it.

In earlier years David often experienced the voices as mocking, telling him that he was worthless or stupid. He still "hears" mocking nonsense phrases, such as "hooyah tooyah, Mr. McGoo-yah." One time he said that they were "trying to make out that I am a total mess." At times he has expressed great anger at the voices, saying that they were "criminal" and that they deserved to be indicted legally. At other times he claims, "They are trying to help me with my handicap." There were periods when David seemed immersed in his voices, using them as a substitute for a (lack of) social life. He now admits that if he had something to do, it would help him not listen to the voices.

He also believes that people around him can read his mind and know what he is thinking, although this belief seemed more insistent at an earlier period. On several occasions he "heard" those around him, such as residents of board-and-care homes where he lived, say disparaging things about him or those close to him. Altercations with residents or staff, sometimes to the point of fisticuffs, occurred on several occasions as a result of such "voice" promptings. In the last year or so, the voices seem to be more benign wish-fulfillment comments or suggestions. For example, David might arrive on the bus for an unscheduled visit to our home, looking pleased with himself that he had managed the trip and declaring that he had heard his father's voice telling him to come. On May 2, 2008, as we were driving home, I told him that I probably could get him an inexpensive second-hand TV to replace the one that had been accidentally smashed by his former roommate. David declared that he had just heard a voice saying, "You have a heart of gold." I asked him whether it was he or I who had a heart of gold, and he replied, "Both of us."

David often reports things the voices tell him as if they were information, prefacing his remarks with the statement that "I heard that. . . ." For example, he has claimed a number of times that the director of a board-and-care home where he formerly lived was seen in a boat off the Los Angeles coast pouring detergent into the ocean. He has reported that this same director was engaged in various nefarious businesses, such as a prostitution ring. A childhood friend whom he has not seen since he was six years old figures prominently in this "voice-information" as someone also engaged in nefarious business. At times David has claimed "information" about his sisters—that one of them is on drugs or the other has separated from her husband. A good friend of mine from Chicago also appears often in this "information." One time he claimed to have heard that she had been pushed from a plane.

Sometimes what David "hears" from a voice simply seems to be what he regards as an interesting "fact." For example, one afternoon he asked if I knew that Miss Taco Supreme lives in El Monte and that she is the daughter of Gabriel Garcia Marquez (a famous Latin American writer). I asked how he knew this. Because he "heard" the voice of Gabriel Garcia Marquez telling him so. How did he know that this was the voice Gabriel Garcia Marquez? Because at an earlier time in his life he had read *One Hundred Years of Solitude* and other works of Gabriel Garcia Marquez.

The next day I pursued the matter by asking David who was Miss Taco Supreme. He said he didn't know but he had seen her name in something he had read. I suggested we look up Miss Taco Supreme on the Internet, but we found no reference to her. I then suggested we look up Gabriel Garcia Marquez to find out more about his life and writing. The Wikipedia account mentioned Marquez's wife and two sons. "Oh," said David, "I guess I was wrong. He doesn't have a daughter."

I continually respond to these statements about voices by saying that they are ideas coming from David's own mind and that they cannot be taken as objective information. When he "hears" disparaging material about his sisters or friends that I think could be harmful to his relations with these people, I say specifically that this information is incorrect. I also encourage him to "push the voices to the back of his mind" or "not to listen to them." When he says that he heard his father's voice telling him to come home, I joke that, "I think this is your own voice, the voice of your wishes." He sometimes grins as if acknowledging that this is the case.

Thus, more recently, David seems to be willing to take this "voice-information" lightly, even to receive a reality check that shows that something he "heard" is not actually happening or being done by these other people. But clearly these voices continue to be compelling experiences for him. He hears them in ways that make him listen and at least half believe what they say to him. Some years ago David even asked me if I could get a priest to perform an exorcism on him, indicating that he seemed to experience the voices as a kind of state of being possessed. This request has not come up recently.

While neuroleptic medication represses the voices some people with schizophrenia hear, in our experience David's hearing of voices has been fairly impervious to medication. Although David's voices seem more benign, they do not seem to have stopped or even to have lessened.

Hearing Voices within Religious Experience:
What Is Acceptable?

Of all the symptoms of schizophrenia, hearing voices is the one that particularly fuzzes over into experiences that are widely shared by "normal"
people. Who has not had a thought "pop into your head" in such a compelling way it is heard as a "voice"? Perhaps what separates the mentally
"ill" from the "well" is being able to recognize this voice as one's own
thought, rather than experiencing it as the voice of someone else.

Another common experience of most humans is dreams that often
contain both vivid visual experiences and conversations between several
parties. Although dreams are no longer seen as coming from God or the
gods, many people continue to see them as important messages coming
from one's unconscious. Even today, dreaming is not seen as something
to be repressed, but rather as important to one's health. REM sleep, or
rapid-eye-movement sleep, which occurs when we dream,[7] is deemed
necessary for a good night's sleep.

Hearing the voices of invisible others is also a common experience in many religious traditions, these invisible others being identified with God, gods, Christ, saints, or angels. The book of Acts reports
that after Jesus had been crucified and buried, his disciples experienced
him as present with them, talking with them, and even sharing a meal
with them. Then Jesus was seen disappearing into the heavens, after
which two angels appeared and told the disciples that he would one day
descend again: "When he had said this, as they were watching, he was
lifted up, and a cloud took him out of their sight. While he was going
and they were gazing up toward heaven, suddenly two men in white
robes stood by them. They said, 'Men of Galilee, why do you stand looking upward toward heaven? This Jesus, who has been taken up from you
into heaven, will come in the same way as you saw him go into heaven'"
(Acts 1:9-11). What distinguishes this crucial religious revelation for
Christians from a visual and auditory hallucination?

Oral tradition may have facilitated the ability to "hear" and recite
long passages of poetic language. Mohammed, the founding prophet of
Islam, heard the angel Gabriel dictate to him the verses of the Qur'an

over a twenty-three year period. He, in turn, recited these verses to
audiences, some of whom became his followers. In these recitations
Mohammed spoke to audiences long accustomed to prophetic utter-
ances by seers and poets who had developed an elegance of language
through long centuries of oral tradition.[8] His followers only gradually
wrote down the verses.

Long revelatory messages continue to be communicated orally to
people regarded as seers today. For example, in the early 1990s I was
given a flyer from someone on the streets of Chicago. The flyer turned
out to be an extended revelation communicated to a woman named
Sister Guadalupe: "Sister Guadalupe is what we call a Seer or Mystic.
From 1988 to 1990 she received messages from the Virgin Mary and
from Christ, our Lord." There followed an extended message from the
Virgin Mary warning all hearers, particularly lay Catholics, of the coming advent of the Antichrist. The coming of this Antichrist was identified particularly with the changes in Catholic practice brought about by
the reforming Second Vatican Council. The message from Mary started
with the words "Dearly beloved children, the Blessed Virgin, Mother
of God, speaks to you through my instrument, my beloved daughter,
Sister Guadalupe. The Holy Spirit and I warn you of the great danger
that threatens you, which is the coming of the Antichrist. My priests and
nuns do not want to listen to my voice nor spread these messages. So I
call on you lay people and on all people who love me to spread them."
Details on this coming chastisement continued for the rest of the page,
ending with the warning that this would happen before the end of the
twentieth century. "There isn't much time left."

Julian Jaynes, in his 1976 book, *The Origin of Consciousness and the
Breakdown of the Bicameral Mind*,[9] saw this experience of voices, identified with gods or revelatory figures, as defining a whole era of early civilization when the key literature of religious traditions, such as the *Iliad*
for ancient Greeks, the Bible for Jews and Christians, and the Qur'an for
Muslims, was written. In the *Iliad*, the action is directed by the gods who
appear as vivid auditory and visual presences in the midst of the battle.

Hearing as well as speaking to God, Jesus, and the saints continued
to be common in Christianity though the Middle Ages and, for some

people, until today. Christian prayer continues to be addressed to God as if speaking to an invisible person who can hear and respond to one's spoken or unspoken words. But it has become more questionable to claim to hear God, Jesus, or the saints speaking to you in return. One recalls Joan of Arc, who was directed by vivid auditory communication with her saints, the angel Michael, Saint Catherine, and Saint Margaret. Neither those who venerated her as an inspired leader nor those who burned her at the stake as a witch doubted that she really heard these voices. Rather, the debate was about whether these voices came from God or the devil.

In his book, Jaynes sought to explain the brain function that underlies such vivid auditory experiences. Human beings have a "double" brain, with a left and a right side. In right-handed persons the speech areas of the brain are all on the left side. But a corresponding area on the right side of the brain has the latent capacity for speech. The two areas communicate by a bridge of fibers. Jaynes speculated that in the earlier era of civilization prior to modern consciousness an array of admonitory, commanding, and insightful messages were formulated in the right side of the brain and communicated to the left speech areas in ways that were "heard" as voices, voices that were interpreted as coming from a divine person (in the context of theocratic societies).[10] Jaynes did not explain why these divine persons were sometimes seen visually and not only heard as voices.

According to Jaynes these more theocratic societies broke down in later antiquity. The distinct individual began to emerge, starting with the elite (males). The "I" began to insert itself between the divine voice coming from the right side of the brain and the obedient servant who heard the voice of the god on the left side of the brain. The individual "I" came to appropriate these voices as "thoughts" within one's own process of consciousness.

The transition between the era of the bicameral mind, where the voice of the gods was vividly heard, and the emergence of modern consciousness, which no longer heard the voices of the gods, was experienced as a time of bewilderment and guilt, when the deities seem to have withdrawn themselves and were no longer available. Gradually the voices fell silent, the individual "I" became dominant, and all that remained of the heard voices of the gods were the recorded scriptures from an earlier era. Disappointingly, Jaynes did not explain what shift in the relation of the two sides of the brain accompanied this breakdown of the bicameral mind and the emergence of individual consciousness.

Whether Jaynes's theory works to explain all aspects of earlier cultures when divine voices were vividly heard can be debated. What is important for the purposes of this exploration is that significant sectors of humans today, particularly those less secularized sectors that still participate in shamanistic and pentecostal forms of religion, continue to have and to cultivate vivid experiences of divine voices and presence.

Anton Boisen, in his 1936 book, *The Exploration of the Inner World: A Study of Mental Disorder and Religious Experience*,[11] detailed the similarity between the classic Protestant evangelical "conversion" experience and the onset of schizophrenic psychosis, both of which tend to take place in late adolescence. In the Protestant conversion experience, intentionally promoted by churches from the sixteenth century to today but less common with liberalization of Protestantism, the individual is assumed to go through a period of extreme emotional troubling sometime between adolescence and adulthood. This emotional troubling puts him or her in touch with what the Calvinist tradition saw as the human condition of "total depravity." The person in this crisis experienced extreme feelings of worthlessness and divine wrath and felt judged by and abandoned by God.

This period of emotional troubling climaxed in a "bottoming out" experience in which one's acute feelings of worthlessness and divine judgment were suddenly and gratuitously reversed by an experience of divine mercy and forgiveness that came directly from God, undeserved and unmediated by human efforts. The individual felt caught up in an ecstatic experience of divine grace, often accompanied by hallucinatory affects, such as voices and lights. The converted person felt assured of God's election of and love for him or her personally. This conversion experience allowed the person to reorganize the meaning of his or her life, adopt a disciplined moral way of living, and join the church and become a hardworking member of society. Often, such conversions included a new sense of personal vocation, a call to ministry, or a new path of life that would both obey God's call and "save the world."

This understanding of the conversion experience allowed generations of Christians to interpret the period of adolescent crisis and use it to guide young people into a new understanding of the meaning of life and their places in it. Today, such a stage of crisis and acute psychosis is met primarily by pathologizing it as mental illness and the prescription of psychiatric medication. As a result, the symptoms may be partly repressed, but the crisis of meaning is unresolved and the emergence of a new organization of the meaning of life and one's purposes in it may not take place. Rather, the person in crisis becomes "stuck" in the permanent status of being one who is "mentally ill."

Another example of such crisis experience and ecstatic transformation is found in various forms of shamanism the world over. Shamanistic religious traditions are characterized by forms of spirit possession, where a divine power takes over the possessed person and uses his or her body to speak to the assembled believers. For example, in Santeria and Condomblé, African-based religions developed in Latin America by African slaves, there is a belief in a multiplicity of orishas, or mediating deities between humans and the high God, Olodumare. This high God does not function directly in human experience. The higher or spirit world is mediated through the orishas.

The orishas are both male and female, young and old, and each has a distinctive identity that represents different personality traits and spheres of activity. Each human person is chosen at birth by an orisha, but gradually becomes aware of who his or her orisha is. Those who become adepts and priest or priestesses go through a crisis, often involving physical and mental illness, until they accept their orisha or acknowledge who "owns one's head." In states of possession, the adept falls into a trance, is taken over by the orisha, and speaks and dances as his or her embodied presence.[12]

Thus the voices of the gods have not fallen silent for many humans living today, but only for certain classes and cultures, particularly those educated in secular society. This suggests that a certain process of cultural socialization teaches people to no longer hear voices or at least not to identify the voices they hear with gods and saints. But there are many subcultures, even within the West, where such experiences are sought after, cultivated, and embraced.

In his popular book *Surviving Schizophrenia*,[13] psychiatrist E. Fuller Torrey claimed that hearing voices or seeing visions is mental illness only when it occurs outside of an established culture that accepts such voices and visions as appropriate or valued. Thus, a person praying to a statue of Mary who hears Mary's voice speaking to her is not mentally ill if her community accepts and values this experience. If, however, one hears such a voice outside a culture that acknowledges and accepts this experience, it is a symptom of illness. By ruling out experiences, such as spirit possession, that occur within cultures that accept and cultivate such experiences as mental illness, Torrey conveniently avoided the suggestion, offensive to believers, that voices and visions that are a part of religious tradition are evidence of "craziness."

But such a distinction between mental illness and sanity in terms of social acceptance or rejection begs the question. Undoubtedly, being rejected and labeled as "crazy" because of hearing voices or seeing visions might contribute to making a person mentally ill. By contrast, a person who falls into trances and speaks as the voice of a divine person in the context of a religion such as Santeria would not only be validated but would secure an honored and lucrative position; Santeria gives such people an esteemed place and role in their community.

This affirmation is undoubtedly good for one's mental and social well-being. But what does this tell us about the functioning of the human brain that results in some people hearing voices? Why is hearing voices a symptom of a "disease" and malfunction of the brain in one social context and evidence of a seer in another? Perhaps the difference is simply that some people have accepting social settings and interpretive frameworks in which to channel such experiences and others do not.

Obsessions and Paranoia, or They Really Are Out to Get You

David has several recurrent themes of thought that I label "obsessions." One of these themes is the idea that he has broken the little finger on his right hand. His little finger, in fact, is not broken and never was broken, although it is somewhat double jointed and deformed by constant twisting. But the thought that his finger was and is broken constantly comes up and seems to be a way of seeking an answer to the question of why he is having problems. David often asks, "When did this happen to me? Was it when I was hit by a bat as a child? Did some childhood friend do this to me?" He often suggests that his inability to function and "get on with his life" is because he has a broken finger. Each time this comes up, I patiently explain that his finger is, in fact, not broken and has never been broken. He receives this opinion in a nonplussed manner. However, in December 2008 he seemed to change his mind. Examining his hands, he announced, "I think Mom is right. There is nothing wrong with my hands."

David also has attributed his ills to deliberate malpractice on the part of various doctors and social workers. Due to a self-induced accident in Illinois, his foot is badly deformed. This causes him to walk in a slightly lopsided manner. He is convinced that the doctors who worked on his shattered leg and foot deliberately set it badly, although doctors who have examined it more recently have spontaneously (not in response to David's question) asserted that it was a remarkably good job, given his injuries. He also broke his hip (another self-induced injury), and he is convinced that the doctor who set it deliberately inserted a bullet into it. Several times he has complained that he has lost part of the back of his head, that his head used to be round in the back and now is flat. He has claimed that the social workers in a program he attended in Los Angeles deliberately performed some kind of "voodoo" (his term) to flatten the back of his head.

David's compulsive flipping behavior, which caused injuries to his elbow, hip, leg, and feet and for which he still bears the scars, seems to have stopped. Perhaps his blaming of his troubles on a finger broken in childhood and medical conspiracies is a way of avoiding taking responsibility for what he has done to himself.

David also speaks often of people stealing things from him. Here it is difficult to separate fact from fiction because it is evident to us that at both the board-and-care homes and at the mental hospitals there is a notorious lack of respect for people's personal belongings and an absence of protection against stealing by others. On many occasions David's personal belongings, which are collected and put in a box for safekeeping when he is admitted to a mental hospital, are not returned to him upon his release. Shoelaces routinely taken from his shoes, out of concern that he could hang himself, never seem to be returned. In several board-and-care homes, clothes, money, watches, heaters, and food have disappeared. David does not seem to obsess very much about these thefts. After initial complaints, he mostly forgets about them. But one obsession that is ongoing is the loss of his "papers." For many years we have given David notebooks and encouraged him to write for mental stimulation and to have something to do in hospitals and board-and-care homes. Over the years he has filled many notebooks, usually writing in pen. When he is in hospitals pens are forbidden; they are considered dangerous weapons, so he writes in pencil. Once he asked for a typewriter. When we got him one, he filled 100 pages with typing in a few days.

I have saved about thirty such collections of David's writings, yet undoubtedly dozens more have been lost over the years. A collection of poems he wrote at Duck Island was left behind when he departed. Cleaning women have thrown out piles of paper on which he had written, and hospitals have discarded such papers when he left.

Even though he still has a lot of his "papers," David feels keenly that he has lost some valuable writing. In one of his hospitalizations, he says, he filled over 100 pages on two stacks of paper, and these were not given to him when he left. Sometimes he suggests that some of this writing was deliberately stolen from him, that it was valuable, that it was worth "a lot of money," and perhaps someone has taken it to publish it. The spectacle of his mother constantly writing and publishing books doubtless feeds this obsession.

Rather than seeing such messages and obsessions as simply "nonsense" and symptoms of a disease, it seems to me important to recognize that they have symbolic significance. Sometimes, when I am able to identify the inner meaning of some idea, David seems satisfied to accept that. For example, in June 2008, David again brought up the idea that a lot of his papers had been stolen and that they were "worth a lot of money." I replied that it is not that easy to get much money from publishing. Serious writing often does not earn very much. But the important thing is that these writings are "valuable to you." David agreed and seemed satisfied with this interpretation.

My recent reading in cognitive-behavioral therapy has helped me formulate this kind of more helpful response to David's obsessions. Cognitive-behavioral therapy is a method of helping people recognize dysfunctional thought patterns and learn how to correct them to prevent emotional reactions of anger, panic, and depression.

There are a number of dysfunctional patterns of "automatic" or spontaneous thought that create negative feelings and behaviors. One of these is "filtering" or isolating a bad element from complex experiences and so condemning the whole. Another is "polarized thinking" or seeing things in good/bad opposites. A third is "overgeneralization" or assuming that one bad experience makes everything bad about a particular person or place. A fourth is "mind-reading" or assuming to know what another person is thinking, usually negative toward oneself. A fifth is "catastrophizing" or assuming one bad experience spells a coming disaster. A sixth is "magnifying" or blowing things out of proportion. A seventh is "personalizing" or setting up a comparison that negates oneself in relation to another. Finally, there are the "shoulds,"[14] which construct rigid rules for oneself that make one upset toward others.

Many of these patterns are similar to the "symptoms" of schizophrenia and depression. Cognitive-behavioral therapy has proven more efficacious than medication in helping many people get beyond dysfunctional thinking simply by identifying these patterns of thought and practicing correcting them in a systematic and practical way on a daily basis. Since these patterns are so widespread and can be helped greatly by cognitive-behavioral training, one wonders in what sense they are symptoms of a "brain disease." Perhaps biological psychiatry needs to take more seriously the statement in the *DSM-IV-TR* that the "positive" symptoms of schizophrenia, that is, voices, delusions, ideas of reference, and paranoia, "appear to reflect an excess or distortion of normal functions."

Incoherent Speech and Poverty of Thought: David's Writings

One of the common "symptoms" of schizophrenia, according to the official psychiatric diagnosis, is confused and incoherent speech and poverty of thought. This is sometimes referred to as a "word salad" of meaningless words and phrases strung together. Schizophrenics are described as suffering from a "poverty of speech."

In high school David had some promise as a writer. During an early period after the onset of his illness (1982), he filled a "dream journal" with articulate and poignant poems and reflections, even though he was largely mute, covering his face with his hands when we tried to get him to talk to us or to psychiatrists. Since that time, as mentioned above, he has engaged in a great deal of writing. Some of this writing has a compelling and somewhat tragic or ironic character. Some seems to be simply lists of rhyming phrases. Some are long discourses that don't seem to add up to any coherent argument, but have many flashes of insight, as if he were engaged in a kind of existentialist reflection on life and language. David's desire to express himself in writing is indicated by the following short piece:

"An Up-standing Probe"

An up-standing probe
As a result of so much passage of time.
The maturing of habits,
Indicative sometimes of damnation.
Essential at times
To a long-standing association
With writer's block
Of the indigestion of Art.
I must find recorded the Act or Plot
To seize my right to be
A man of letters.

David still retains some fluency in Spanish vocabulary and grammar and will often write long discourses or short "poems" entirely in Spanish. Following is one of many short pieces he has written. It seems to be a kind of "dream journey," which he has titled "With a Good Wish for the

Demon." It speaks of a "stranger" who "knows how to designate difficult waves in time or perhaps in the earth." "From his childhood there
arose the need for adventure. His idea is to go on grand excursions in
the night and then return in the morning by the light of the stars." His
"enchantment" was with a movement of the moon, going by foot, when
he came to know that "the price of the journey is infinite."

"Con Felicidad para el Demonio"

Un forastero conoce el tipo designado
Para designar las ondas difíciles
En el tiempo,
O, tal vez, en la tierra.
Desde su niñez surge la necesidad
Para adventura.
Su idea es que puede ir
Para grandes excursiones
En la noche y entonces revolver
Por la luz de las estrellas.
En la manaña de la manaña
Su onoontamionto ora porque
De un movimiento de la luna
Cuando todo estaba
Persiguiendose de ir por pie
Entonces el entendimiento
Que el precio de peregrinación
Es infinito.

Although prone at times to malapropism—making up words—David
also has a capacity to spell (real) words accurately. There have been times
when David has fallen into incoherent speech or even an inability to
speak at all, but mostly the way he writes is different from the way he
speaks. His speech is mostly matter of fact and even insightful about his
surroundings. He has a playful sense of humor, and he is often able to
receive our efforts to disabuse him of his voices or fantasies thoughtfully.

His more matter-of-fact style of daily speech is reflected in the many
letters he wrote me while I was teaching in Berkeley, California, from

2002 to 2005. I stayed in Berkeley during the week, coming home on weekends and holidays. He wrote the following letter about September 2002, shortly after he had been ejected from the first board-and-care home in Claremont and moved to another one, "Holy Care"—so called because it was a former convent—in El Monte, California.

Dear Mom,

I am getting used to Holy Care and today I find myself enjoying the "time" more than usual.

Today, so far, I went out and bought coffee and just tried to ignore some of these "persisting memories." Soon, it will be dinner time and I am anxious to see how I will be feeling tonight!

My room remains my ultimate concourse. I sidle out of it every so often, but it remains a bit "cooler" than every where else.

Yesterday Dad came for the first time and we walked around the "Hood". He bought me some house slippers, this notebook I am writing on and some bug-spray to get rid of the ants that emerge at times.

Tomorrow I will be going to the program at the Hospital and I will try to not be upset because of my twisted finger which seems to be my major shortcoming toward my involvements in life.

Once again I hope to thank you for buying me my own T.V. set and maybe someday I will get a bicycle.

I still drink a lot of water and seem to swallow excessively and do occasionally regurgitate because of all these recessive tendencies. Today, though, the daughter of the cook and the "janitor" gave me a stack of half decent drawing paper as a sort-of gift.

So, all in all, things could be worse were I still in the Claremont Care. So all I have to do is to try to moderate myself to the pensive side and I should be alright.

Yesterday Dad gave me ten dollars which, of course, will disappear like hot cakes. . . But we got to see a small part of the neighborhood, and it seems to be a generally congenial and attractive place, with a predominantly Hispanic touch and the average cohabitation of Filipinos.

So thanks for your letter and greetings from Berkeley, and I will try to capture a little more of the right example from day to day.

Love,
David

His dozens of short writings or poems express David's more allusive use of language and untutored gift of rhythm. The following poems illustrate this kind of language.

"A Primal Tunnel"

A primal tunnel
Drained of all energy
Spent and derailed
Departed from reality.
Difficult and exhaled
Attached to malignity.

Sedated and exposed,
Apprehended by penalty
Distanced by pride
The disposition of ferocity.
To be related toward its kind,
An essential difficulty.

Parlayed from antipathy
Explosive arguments
Raised through adversity
Swollen particles
Embodied with dexterity,
Seeking an outlet.

"Crying Hours"

Crying hours
The cold singularity
Of emptiness,
Dark and completely distended
Dementia dropping unaware
Into stillness.
Yearning for release
From the dismal times.

Mediocre signs
Upon the mantle
Of calculated madness

And differing moods
Infernal interludes
Of broken staffs,
Straddled lines
At the zone of danger.

The melancholy deeps
And drying spores,
Manhandling examples
Of deplorable recreation,
Shunted occasions
Of irreverent dismissal
A decisive act
Of mortal distress.

"A Slave to Sleep"

A slave to sleep
Living on the break-up
At border line of
Night and day.
A nocturnal dependency,
Nearness to the dark.

A hole into which to climb,
Day after day
Turning off the lights,
The burying of grief and emotion,
Ungratefully or, so to speak,
Imprisoned in the waking dead.

Declining to care
About the destiny of selfishness,
The occurrence of abandonment,
The call of banality.

As an example of David's more extended prose, I excerpt some passages from a twelve-page typed writing that he titled "On the Average." It expresses his anger with and alienation from the mental health system. The language is somewhat chaotic, allusive, yet hardly just a "word salad" of meaningless phrases. Far from a "poverty of language," the vocabulary is rich and complex, and there is a striving to express a vision of how things should be in contrast to destructive social systems. It was written in 2004 during one of his many hospitalizations in the psychiatric hospital in the Hawthorne area of Los Angeles.

The populace or the world at large constitute the whole throng or multitude of concerned parties who want to acknowledge the presence of a guiding spirit or light from within. The persuasive power or persisting presence of such a wide majority of a huge continuum of protective and directly connected beings who are discreetly interdependent, mainstays supporting the backbone or constitution of the system which survives to tell the story of a growing movement of freely associated positive thinking correspondents who are learning to apply themselves to the greatest task of all, parlaying free excitability to a world where complacent peer groups appeal vainly for their dances of prestige.

Nobody really gets acquainted with authority figures who get all excited about nothing. People can tolerate authority, but you cannot satisfy anything remarkable with little nitty, stingy voices, because nobody gets acquainted or minds the business of technology. In my case I don't tolerate technology because I prefer to think independently and would prefer to preserve some inkling of sanity or reverence for the altruistic or refined construct model which I think God created. Anyone could relate irately or with some petty allowance for selectivity or even preaching some strange doctrine of freedom. Not withstanding that we always search for sobriety, there is the stalemate or indignity of suffering from schizophrenia, all because you constantly admit or confess your need for comfort zones or character builders. I guess the real achievement or challenge is to accomplish something worth sharing. And, of course, resignation to duty will always compel us to "believe" in whatever we are disposed to, as a contrivance or of some singularity. But since the motive stays the same every day, I think one must be braced for time by way of being with it or behaving according to some fashion or recognizable characteristic. This is what we are brought up to believe, that there is relevance in life.

The reason why schizophrenia can be satisfactory, as opposed to some awful sickness, is a matter of having in mind that everyone has

*an ailment which some poltergeist is trying to take away. The pres-
ent strife is concerted in the vain effort of some spokespersons who
are of the mistaken criterion or creed that some managerial quality is
found in confused and ridiculous coverage by the media and an inter-
fering voice-related condescension. What it amounts to is a scheme
or unscholarly creed of some very ridiculous tendency toward circu-
lating a dumb contagion of so-called sentiments expressed by these
totally absurd factions whose goal or god is complete blindness and
unauthorized voice-manipulation.*

*The true calumny is quite obvious. These people have always been
addicted to their innocuous pleas for popularity. And they think that
they have counterparts within the corrupt system. I do think there is a
concept which is not trying to criticize these inflammatory sources of
confusion and maladjustment, but only trying to put across how tire-
some it is, when the enlarged or more refined crescendo of life gets all
loused up by the very same contagion. The pulse or intended rhythm
and time of life is put asunder by any fool who thinks that thought can
make all sorts of constant comments. Breaking it up with some strange
allusion of consistency is always a good objective. But how to simply
appeal smacks of the tragedy. And I do not consider it sick. I think it
is our god-given right to be preoccupied. And impulse control is not
enough. You must bear witness or testify to your intelligence, if you
have any. But my discontent is an effort to contradict even whatever
is possibly "my problem," so that the persistence of emotion will carry
through and follow through to fortify and designate the exchanges and
stages which contribute to a totality. I am convinced it will help as
long as the thread of recovery contributes to a totality.*

Passivity and Loss of Drive: Disease, Drugs, or Learned Dependence?

The official psychiatric description of the signs of schizophrenia include
the "negative symptoms" of loss of motivation—loss of ability to work,
organize one's life, and care for oneself. Some of this has been the case
with David. One of the most frustrating and discouraging effects of
David's illness over the last three decades has been a loss of drive, a
loss of the ability to create an organized plan of life and to work toward

accomplishing goals in any systematic way. It is not that he has lost all motivation for education, work, and self-betterment. He often speaks of "getting his life together" and expresses a keen desire for a job and to have his own car and apartment. But what it would mean to accomplish these goals seems largely to escape him.

It has been almost thirty years since David has held a paying job, and those he held in his youth were of the teenage variety—cooking in a restaurant, room service in a hotel, and a couple of menial park-service jobs raking leaves. He basically has lost work skills and discipline. Even though he has done some work in mental health communities, such as Duck Island, Gould Farm, and Kahumana, this was in the early days of his illness. The board-and-care homes where he has been a resident since 1989 have lacked completely any work component or even the effort to get residents to clean their rooms, much less help around the grounds. Nor have the mental health clinics he has frequented had any access to work programs, with the exception of Thresholds in Chicago, where work was an integral part of the program.

When David expresses the desire for a job, I try to remind him of what a regular job entails: getting up regularly, being clean and well dressed, getting to the job on time, and being able to concentrate and work efficiently for eight hours. This clearly is well beyond his present capacities. So I suggest that he start with part-time or volunteer work to prepare for more full-time work. With this in mind, David and I have volunteered in the Beta Center in Pomona, a food bank for people who are poor and homeless, run by the Pomona Valley Council of Churches. David is great at carrying food from the storage room and stacking it according to type in the room where the orders are filled, but his ability to work depends entirely on my giving him constant direction: "David, take this box of soup cans to the dispensary," and so on. The ability to discern what needs to be done and to set about doing it himself seems beyond him. He soon loses energy and stands around or sits down. So too, when his father tries to get him to help with the vegetable garden or cleaning the patio. David can help for a few minutes, and then he disconnects. He seldom takes the initiative to see what needs to be done and sets about doing it. The exception is the kitchen, where he seems to have some idea of what needs to be done; here he sometimes will ask if he can cut the vegetables for the meal, or he gets up to clear the table and help wash dishes.

David is not without some self-care skills. After I bought him an electric shaver (to prevent him cutting himself with a razor) to keep in our home (so it wouldn't get lost or broken at the board-and-care home), he regularly goes into the bathroom and shaves when he visits our house and also brushes his teeth after dinner. Although he has a toothbrush and toothpaste in his room and claims he brushes his teeth at his residence, I suspect this seldom happens.

Through regular four- to five-hour visits to our home on Tuesdays, Fridays, and Sundays, we see to David's basic cleanliness and some regular recreation. We wash his dirty clothes and keep most of his clothing in boxes in a closet at our home. During his visits, he changes his underwear and socks and outer garments from these boxes. Clearly, we are holding up most of the job of keeping him clean and well clothed. It would be better for him to do all these things where he is living. But the board-and-care home offers such chaotic services that we resort to doing these things at our home. This means what we do for him in the family is contributing to his dependence. But we are at a loss to find better ways for him to take responsibility for these tasks of daily life for himself.

The board-and-care home provides David's meals and doles out his medications, with which he has generally been compliant, despite his negative views of medication. Since the meals are highly starchy and lack rounded nutrition, we see that he has fruit juices with him and some other healthy snacks. He uses the money given to him by the state ($20 a week) mainly to go out and purchase innutritious food, such as donuts, Cokes, and hamburgers. Thus, David functions at a level of extreme dependence, both in his residence and at home with us.

Is this extreme dependency and lack of self-organizational capacity a "symptom" of his disease? The psychiatric diagnostic manuals would have one believe that it is, although the *DSM-IV-TR* also hints it may be caused by medication and environmental "understimulation." Not all schizophrenics exhibit such lack of drive. In her remarkable biography, *The Center Cannot Hold,* Elyn Saks[15] describes her most harrowing experiences of threatening inner messages and dangerous "acting out," such as dancing on roofs of buildings. As a result she was hospitalized repeatedly both in England and in the United States. Yet, through it all she never lost her determined drive and managed to complete advanced degrees in classics and in law. While continuing to experience symptoms of schizophrenia controlled by medication, she has had a successful law career combined with work in psychiatric counseling. She has published numerous books and articles that bring together law and mental illness.[16]

Saks is exceptional in her ability to carry on her education and career at a high level while experiencing the most debilitating effects of mental illness. She herself has come to accept that medication is necessary to control the worse symptoms, but she believes that her work in psychoanalysis, or "talk therapy," is also indispensable to her ability to continue to function. By contrast, contemporary biologically oriented psychiatry seems to have entirely jettisoned "talk therapy" for persons with mental illness, reserving it for the educated, rich "worried well," who have the money, leisure, and articulateness for such a pursuit.[17]

I am not convinced that David's extreme dependency and lack of drive are simply symptoms of a biologically based "disease." They also seem to be connected with the fact that he has been cut out of access to work for almost three decades in a mental health system that seems primarily concerned with pacifying "consumers" and providing drugs, food, and marginal entertainment, but with no work or demands for participation in community maintenance. This surely is stultifying and seems to me a major cause of creating a learned dependency. One can only wonder where David would be today if he had been able to continue at a place like Gould Farm, which had a strong built-in work program.

One also has to ask whether the medications David has been given over these last decades have not had something of a "lobotomizing" effect, as he himself suggests in another excerpt from his writing "On the Average":

The strongest medicine in the world is Haldol Decononait. That is, because it has no function whatsoever. It is merely a contradictor or far-ranging placebo which sticks all over your nerves and makes you hallucinate, being as the brain is being cut off electrically. So your circuit is dead for that reason. The retarded motion of brain activity is what doctors crave, for all the manifestations of organic brain waves to be cut at the base and never connected with brain cells such that people use for communication. Memory, drawing conclusions and hallucinating, "brownouts" or whatever you call them are also affected.

I guess that some people make their living that way, like the doctors. I consider them to be disabling professions, just like psychology and social workers, and I think that the reason why our country is so overrun with hospitals and places of internment, like half-way houses, is equally invalid. They think that nobody experiences a brownout or blackout, with all this marvelous medication. This is the subject because there damn well is a difference between patients and staff. And the real disgrace is that the staff is completely ignorant in spite of their proffered health, if the patients did not notice every nuance of why the medication is a big farce and any institution could do just as well without it, except maybe aspirin. I think the staff members are discourteous and all convinced that they are doing a good job, whereas the patients display reasoning all the time, which is just so typical.

Certainly David has regressed in many basic skills and is now in some ways behind where he was when he was twelve or even younger. David learned to drive a car when he was fourteen, and at seventeen he drove our Volkswagen with his older sister as a passenger from Washington, D.C., to Evanston, Illinois, with perfect competence. Today I would not be willing to let him to drive my car around the block.

What has happened to him to generate such dependency and regression in basic skills in the last thirty years? Is it only some defect in his brain, such as overactive neurotransmitters, as the biological psychiatrists would have us believe, or does the medication itself, combined with a regime of prolonged passivity and dependency, help create this regression? Perhaps no one at this time knows the answer, but at least it needs to be honestly discussed.

Causes of Schizophrenia
Mind, Body, or Both Together?

Theories of the causes of schizophrenia and other forms of mental illness have varied over the centuries in Western thought; so also have the
proposed cures. Although we are tempted to assume that this question
is over and we now have definite scientific knowledge of what causes
schizophrenia, current theories continue to be contested. The lack of
good "cures" itself drives the ongoing debate. The supposition is that if
we really knew what caused schizophrenia, we should be able to cure
it, or at least alleviate its symptoms more fully. Thus, it is useful to look
at earlier theories to see how certain patterns of argument continually
reoccur.

This debate reflects a perennial dualism in Western thought between
mind and body. Is mental illness caused primarily by social-psychic factors, such as poor childrearing, bad moral formation, or experiences of
trauma in the process of social development? Or is it primarily physiological or somatic defects that can be remedied by medicines or surgery? Variants of this argument have flowed back and forth for at least
two hundred years and were particularly intense in the 1960s, when
those with a psychoanalytic focus vied with those recommending brain
surgery or electroconvulsive shock therapy.

This debate between psychic and somatic causes and remedies has also been deeply intertwined with the professional prestige of psychiatrists. Are psychiatrists modern secular heirs of a religious tradition of soul-cure in which an expert on the complex processes of mental, moral, and spiritual life guides the psyche to heal itself of destructive thoughts and feeling and to develop the good self? From at least the mid-nineteenth century, psychiatrists sought to escape the heritage of being a soul-guide, and to ally themselves with science and medicine as a scientific specialty. To find physical causes and hence physical cures was to vindicate psychiatry as medicine based on science.

Colonial America: Demons or Blood Humors?

From Christian tradition and from Greek medicine, colonial America inherited two very different theories of mental illness, one spiritual and the other somatic. Is mental illness demonic possession? Or is it caused by imbalance of the humors of the blood? The theory of demonic possession has a long history in Christianity. In the New Testament Jesus functioned as an exorcist driving out evil spirits that possessed people. The descriptions of some of the demoniacs healed by Jesus sounds strikingly like severe schizophrenia. Thus, in the account of the Gerasene demonic, Mark 5:2-5 reads:

> And when he [Jesus] had stepped out of the boat, immediately a man out of the tombs with an unclean spirit met him. He lived among the tombs; and no one could restrain him any more, even with a chain; for he had often been restrained with shackles and chains, but the chains he wrenched apart, and the shackles he broke in pieces; and no one had the strength to subdue him. Night and day among the tombs and on the mountains he was always howling and bruising himself with stones.

Jesus commanded the unclean spirit to come out of the man. He then asked the man his name, and the man replied, "My name is Legion; for we are many" (Mark 5:9), suggesting that he was possessed of multiple unclean spirits. Jesus drove these unclean spirits out of the man into a herd of 2,000 swine that then rushed down the hill and were drowned. When the townspeople came out to see what had happened, they found demoniac "sitting there, clothed and in his right mind" (Mark 5:15; compare Luke 8: 26-39 and also Matthew 8:28-34, where there are two demoniacs).

Although today mental illness as demonic possession might appear a totally retrograde idea, schizophrenics who hear many voices that taunt and denigrate them might still think of themselves as "possessed" by evil spirits. Early on in David's illness, he hit on the idea that he was possessed and asked me if I could get a priest who could exorcize him. I knew no exorcist, nor was I about to seek one out, but that David seized on this idea surprised and intrigued me. I had no idea where he got the idea of exorcism. Recently I asked him and found out that he got it from popular culture. Exorcism was a popular theme in movies at the time, with the film *The Exorcist* in 1973 and several sequels in the later 1970s. David saw two of these movies.

The New Testament accounts of Jesus healing demoniacs treat such persons with compassion. They are seen as victims of powers beyond their control, yet the existence of such demonic possession was understood as signs of the reign of the devil in human affairs. In a dispute with the Pharisees who claimed that Jesus cast out demons by the power of the devil, Jesus proclaimed that Satan could not cast out demons since they belonged to his realm. Only one who represented the true God could cast out demons. Jesus' healing work as an exorcist thus represented the dawn of God's reign, breaking the reign of the devil in human history. "But if it is by the Spirit of God that I cast out demons, then the kingdom of God has come to you" (Matt. 12:28).

But colonial America had inherited a tradition of witch-hunting in which those possessed by "demons" were seen as culpable for their "madness," having sold their souls to the devil for some reprehensible gain of power, wealth, or sexual license. Shackling and beating were appropriate responses to those possessed of demons, while those suspected of causing such possession were liable to execution by burning, drowning, or hanging.

A different theory of mental and physical illness came from Greek medicine, which believed that bodily and mental health depended on a balance of the four humors or bodily fluids—phlegm, red blood, yellow bile, and black bile—all based on the blood that was derived from digestion. Extreme anger was caused by excess yellow bile, and melancholy by excess black bile. A phlegmatic lack of energy was believed to be caused by too much phlegm. Bleeding and leeching the body were seen as cures of such excesses, restoring the balance between humors.[1]

Madness was also seen as caused by moral, especially sexual, depravity. In Christian culture, masturbation and sexual indulgence were believed to bring on madness,[2] while sexual self-discipline had long been associated with rationality—the dominance of reason over the appetites. This was reinforced by the Enlightenment, a period when people prized rule of mind over irrational instinct. From this it was a short step to assuming that persons with mental illness were people who had regressed to animal irrationality. The appropriate response was to break such people by beating, as one would break a wild animal. Thus, colonial America inherited a medical theory that suggested a physical cure through bloodletting, while its view of those with mental illness as demoniacs and wild animals disposed them to punitive physical abuse, particularly for those who were unruly.

1800–1950: Bad Moral Formation or Brain Lesions?

The late eighteenth and early nineteenth centuries saw the dawn of a new theory about the cause of mental illness: it was the result of bad moral formation in the family and society. Reformers were horrified by abuse of those with mental illness who were shackled, beaten, and left in filth and rags in hospital prisons for the insane. For them such abuse simply accelerated the regression of the ill to the status of subhumanity. They proposed instead the development of asylums as institutions of moral reeducation. Humane treatment of those with mental illness would rehumanize them and enable them to recover their humanity.

Although one historian of the treatment of mental illness in America referred to the development of asylums as the "medicalization of insanity,"[3] the moral reformers did not actually see insanity as a medical problem and did not speculate about possible physical diseases as its cause. Rather, their focus was on moral reeducation to create internalized self-discipline. One such reformer was the Frenchman Philippe Pinel, who in the late eighteenth century became famous for striking off the chains that fettered those with mental illness in the Salpetriere, the Parisian hospital for the insane. Pinel suggested that various social stresses such as precipitous economic loss, overwork, unrequited love or jealousy, religious fanaticism, or failures in overweening ambition might cause the mind to become "imbalanced."[4] Another reformer was the English Quaker William Tuke, who founded the York Retreat in 1792 for insane members of the Society of Friends.[5]

These advocates of "moral treatment" of "the insane" stressed a combination of firm social order and kindness to restore "the insane" to their "right mind." By implication this capacity for a "right mind" was not absent or irreparably damaged because of some incurable disease. The mind's potential remained at the core of the human nature of every person, but it had been thrown off balance by social stresses or lack of adequate family training due to bad conditions in childhood, such as alcoholism, promiscuity, and disorder. Key to recovery was the removal of the mentally imbalanced person from the social conditions that caused the problem—namely, an undisciplined family and disordered social environment—into a "refuge" (the original idea behind the word *asylum*) where a morally self-disciplined self could redevelop.

Such an asylum would preferably be located in a peaceful rural setting, far from chaotic urban life, where amid the beauties of nature the person could regain inner peace. The regime of the asylum was to have all the characteristics of a well-ordered household on a larger scale. The inmates would arise punctually in the early morning, setting about a routine of work, nutritious meals, cleanup, exercise, education, and elevating recreation at fixed hours. The theory was not libertarian but what might be described as enlightened paternalism. The head of the asylum should be a kindly, all-wise, and also all-controlling father who would retrain the insane in the habits of a well-ordered life.[6]

This theory of moral treatment still partook of the idea that "the insane" were "wild" and needed "breaking," but now in the kindly manner of paternal parenting rather than the violent manner of those breaking horses. In Pinel's words, "One of the major principles of the psychologic management of the insane is to break their will in a skillfully timed manner without causing wounds or imposing hard labor. Rather a formidable show of terror should convince them that they are not free to pursue their impetuous willfulness and that their only choice is to submit."[7] Such a theory of the retraining of "the insane" was thus closely connected with a view of how children should be raised to internalize self-discipline in a proper patriarchal household.

Needless to say such a vision of moral retraining of "the insane" was only possible (if at all) with carefully chosen small groups of people and with adequate funds to create pleasant housing in a rural setting, a high ratio of staff to patients, and a paternal director who put his whole life into his relation to the "family." But the reality was that asylums, with few exceptions, lacked the conditions for such high-quality, intensive care. Patients grew in numbers, the size of asylums expanded to hundreds and even thousands, the staff-patient ratio widened, and funds were not present for decent cleanliness or repairs or well-trained staff, and so such institutions soon degenerated into prisons whose primary purpose was custodial control.

The heads of such institutions for the "insane," the basis of that profession that became psychiatry, were originally called the Association of Medical Superintendents of American Institutions for the Insane.[8] These so-called alienists chafed at being labeled mere institutional managers whose primary job was custodial care for patients and maintaining minimum standards of repair and cleanliness of buildings that always teetered on the edge of being revealed as "hell-holes." They longed to be scientific, to be ranked as real doctors, and hence to have a theory of the somatic roots of mental illness, which lent itself to medical interventions that held out some promise of cure.

But psychiatry in the late nineteenth and early twentieth centuries lacked any clear theory of the biological cause of mental illness. A variety of therapies were practiced, some inherited from humor theory, such as bleeding and hydrotherapy, but their connection with the biological causes of mental illness was uncertain. German psychiatrist Emil Kraepelin (1856–1926) in the late nineteenth century carefully observed the case histories of asylum patients and created categories that tied symptoms to predicted outcomes. He believed that those with manic-depressive illness could hope to get better, but those with dementia praecox (premature dementia, later renamed schizophrenia) could expect only to deteriorate permanently. Kraepelin postulated that a specific brain or other biological pathology lay behind each psychiatric disorder, but he could not specify what these might be. Kraepelin's categories had to do entirely with descriptions of collections of symptoms, not a theory of causes, and this remains the primary basis for diagnosis of mental illness today.[9]

In order to give some scientific basis to their diagnosis, psychiatrists began to speak of mental illness as caused by "brain lesions," but the exact meaning of this term remained unknown. At that time there was no way to examine a living brain. Brains could only be examined in autopsies of the dead, and examination of the brains of deceased mental patients did not disclose consistent evidence of differences between the brains of persons suffering from mental illness and those of healthy people.[10]

Some psychiatrists became convinced that bacterial infections were to blame. The most notorious of these was Henry Cotton, who ruled Trenton State Hospital for the Insane from 1907 until 1930. Cotton became convinced that insanity was caused by bacterial infection in the teeth, tonsils, and colon, and he proceeded to remove all the teeth of his patients, followed by removal of tonsils, colons, gall bladders, and the cervices and ovaries of women, and the castration of men. Despite a high level of deaths and few real recoveries, such operations continued at Trenton until 1960.[11]

The 1930s to 1960s incorporated a variety of physical therapies into the repertoire of "care" in mental hospitals. These included various forms of shock or trauma therapy, such as introducing malaria germs to create a fever, injecting insulin to induce a coma, and administering metrazol (a form of camphor) or electric shock to create a seizure. How creating fever or shock in patients alleviated the symptoms of mental illness was unclear. The idea seemed to be that by bringing the patient back to a comatose state the brain might spontaneously reorganize itself in a calmer, more pliable way. It was admitted that these forms of induced convulsion created brain damage, lessening higher intelligence or destroying parts of the memory, but that many patients seemed "quieter" was regarded as sufficient "cure."[12]

The most direct assault on the brain in order to "cure" or at least relieve the more unruly symptoms of mental illness was lobotomy (see chapter 4 for fuller discussion). A great variety of surgical ways of damaging the brain developed, such as cutting the tissue between the frontal lobes, cutting out parts of the frontal lobes, injecting alcohol to damage the brain, and freezing or burning parts of the brain.[13] The frontal lobes were seen as the seat of intelligence. By damaging parts of it, lobotomists speculated that the excess angers and emotions conveyed to the rest of the brain were relieved.

Lobotomy and the various shock therapies seemed to be physical interventions in search of a causal theory. One began experimentally, often accidentally, with evidence that a particular practice lessened symptoms, and then speculated as to why it "worked." Often, simply "calming" patients—making some percentage of them less unruly and more pliable—was sufficient to declare a procedure a success. That many died or were made worse was dismissed as unimportant compared with the few who were deemed to have gotten "better," that is, able to leave the overcrowded mental hospital to return home, even if returning home simply meant full-time dependency on the family.

A series of cultural assaults on asylum medicine developed in the 1950s and 1960s. Freudian psychoanalysis proposed a provocative theory of the psychosocial origins of mental illness, which challenged the puritan morality of the family. Other theorists began to speculate that mental illness originated primarily in psychosocial conflicts in the family or in society or even that mental disturbance did not really exist as an illness, but rather the definition of it as an illness was a form of social control of cultural deviance imposed by society.

Those searching for physical theories of the causes of mental illness and medical cures were deeply threatened and angered by these challenges. The war between psychoanalytic and somatic theories of the causes of mental illness still echo in the literature today. Psychiatric leaders of the 1930s, such as Adolf Meyer, while deeply interested in finding somatic causes and cures of mental illness, were open to a combination of physical and environmental theories.[14] However the "cultural wars" over the meaning of mental illness of the 1960s deepened the split between psychological-social theories and somatic theories of causes of mental illness that is only beginning to be overcome today.

1950–1970: Refocus on Psyche, Family, and Society

The 1950s to 1970s saw a major refocusing in American psychiatry on psychic trauma and its social roots, especially in conflicts in the family. An important influence in this shift is the thought of Sigmund Freud (1856–1939). Although Freud was not against theories of the somatic roots of psychological conflicts and trained originally as a neurologist, the effect of his thought was to focus on the development of the psyche in its family context, not brain pathology, as the cause of mental illness. For psychoanalysis, "talk therapy" was the primary path of recovery.

Freud's views challenged both the puritanical view of family relations and the Enlightenment's faith in rationality. For Freud, consciousness was a precarious truce between the impulses (the id) and the moral strictures imposed by society (the superego). Freud saw the child as consumed by impulses, particularly sexual desires. According to Freud, society imposed taboos against incest and thus the child learned to repress sexual desires—the girl for her father, the boy for his mother—but these repressions then became the basis for neurotic thoughts and behavior. The cure according to Freud was a long process of "talk therapy," guided by a skilled psychoanalyst who helped the neurotic adult to uncover the memory of these repressed desires and integrate them into conscious self-knowledge, while at the same time strengthening the ego's acceptance of the moral strictures of the superego. Thus, the mature self became freed of neurotic repression by acknowledging its secret desires but at the same time accepting their conscious control.[15]

Although Freud's thought was known in America from 1909, when he first visited here, he became widely popular throughout American culture primarily in the 1950s to 1970s. Many academic departments of psychology in universities became primarily Freudian. Many psychiatrists who had sought to promote a somatic theory of mental illness as rooted in brain pathology to be remedied by shock therapy or psychosurgery were horrified by the new focus on the psychiatrist as soul guide through talk therapy.[16]

Those concerned with the fate of the masses with chronic mental illness in hospitals felt side-stepped by the new emphasis on psychoanalysis. Freud himself never treated schizophrenics or others with severe mental illness, and his methods applied primarily to affluent, well-educated, and articulate neurotics, not to those with severe illness. Psychoanalytically trained psychiatrists now had a major new source of income through well-paid sessions of private counseling, which allowed them to ignore the inarticulate denizens of mental hospitals.

The 1960s saw the popularization of several thinkers who have been dubbed the leaders of the "antipsychiatry" movement, although none of them embraced this term for themselves. One of these was psychiatrist Thomas Szasz, author of *The Myth of Mental Illness* (1960).[17] Szasz was a strict libertarian who objected to any imposition of social controls that limited a person's right to make private choices in matters that did not harm others, such as the consumption of psychedelic drugs or the decision to commit suicide.

Operating with a dogmatic dualism between what was mental and what was biological, Szasz challenged the definition of unconventional mental constructs and behaviors as "mental illness." For Szasz, to define something as an illness or disease must be based on a demonstrable physical defect. Psychiatry had not been able to demonstrate that there was any biological defect that lay behind what is defined as mental illness. An illness that was purely mental was thus a contradiction in terms, one that turned on a confusion of metaphors, like calling a "heartbreak" an illness of the heart.

Szasz also saw any effort to define thought and behavior patterns that were outside the norms of society as illness, and the claims of the state and the mental health establishment to impose coercive measures on such deviant thought and behavior, through such measures as involuntary hospitalization, coerced shock treatment, or lobotomy, as a violation of basic human rights. According to Szasz people should be hospitalized and given psychiatric services only if they themselves agree to them and contract for this.

Another formative skeptic of the medical and psychiatric establishment was French philosopher Michel Foucault, author of *Madness and Civilization* and *The Birth of the Clinic*.[18] Foucault saw the definition of the "mad" by society as an expression of a lineage of exclusion of certain categories of people as outside the norm, like lepers in the Middle Ages. Particularly with the Enlightenment, the "mad" were defined as the "others" to be excluded in a society defined by "reason." The creation of asylums, including the "moral treatment" developed by Philippe Pinel and Samuel Tuke, expressed efforts to both exclude those who didn't conform to the dominant forms of reason and to gather them in a separate controlled space where they would be forced to internalize those norms of reason by coercive training and discipline.

A third influential leader of the critique of established psychiatry of the time was Scot psychiatrist R. D. Laing, author of such books as *The Divided Self* and *Sanity, Madness, and the Family*.[19] Laing contested the view that the language of schizophrenics was meaningless babble. For him such language reflected valid efforts to communicate in conflicting situations where people adopted a personal system of symbolism. Laing believed that rather than dismis such language, psychiatrists should listen to it carefully in order to understand the meaning behind the symbolism within the context of that individual's life.

Laing also belonged to a school of psychiatric thought that saw the etiology of mental illness in deep conflicting relations within the family. Families were seen as pathological systems that forced all their members to repress and deny what they knew about each other for the sake of family "peace." Under this school of thought, the whole family system colluded in these lies, but one person may be particularly victimized. Such "double binds" in the family Laing saw as the root of defining a victimized member of the family as mentally ill. Like Szasz, Laing understood calling this person "mentally ill" as resting on a false episte-mology; illness was defined by deviant behavior or thought patterns but treated as though it rested on a biological defect.

The critical perspectives on psychiatry represented by these think-ers were popularized and oversimplified in the 1960s and 1970s. The ex-patient movement (an organized group of former mental patients) found in such views a justification for their feeling that they had been unjustly abused in mental hospitals.[20] Lawyers defending the human rights of those with mental illness crusaded against any involuntary hos-pitalization or treatment.[21] The impression that those called "mentally ill" were primarily victims of the madness of society, not themselves mad, was widely accepted by those with little experience in chronic mental illness. Theories, such as the "schizophrenogenic mother," were casually adopted to stigmatize parents, and particularly mothers, as the "cause" of the mental illness of a child,[22] with little understanding of the burden such an idea placed on the families of persons with mental ill-ness struggling to help their afflicted members.

1970 to Today: Back to the Broken Brain

However, those favoring a somatic explanation of mental illness and the quest for medical solutions to it were not slow in fighting back against this attack on psychiatry as scientifically based medicine. This was aided by the development of antipsychotic drugs in the 1950s.

The first neuroleptic drug to be marketed in the United States was chlorpromazine (Thorazine) in 1954.[23] It was first synthesized in France in 1950 as a numbing agent during surgery, where it was dis-covered to create an emotional detachment that made patients dis-interested in what was going on around them. One of its developers referred to it as a "veritable medicinal lobotomy." It was then used to calm mental patients at St. Anne's Hospital in Paris. Thorazine was early recognized to induce the symptoms of Parkinson's disease, char-acterized by a shuffling gait and a masklike face. It was introduced into mental asylum medicine primarily as a substitute for lobotomy, to cre-ate a calming of agitated patients.[24]

It was in the mid-1950s to early 1960s that Thorazine underwent a marketing image makeover that touted it as a "miracle cure" for schizophrenia, which would enable states to empty their mental hospitals and send patients into community care where they could receive the drug through outpatient services from neighborhood clinics, a vision that reflected President John F. Kennedy's plan to reform care for persons afflicted with mental illness in the United States. As Kennedy put it, the new drugs would make it "possible for most of the mentally ill to be successfully and quickly treated in their own communities and returned to a useful place in society."[25]

The claims of future success led researchers to ask how the new drug worked. In 1963 Swedish pharmacologist Arvid Carlsson showed that Thorazine inhibited the transmission of messages between the cells of the brain by repressing the chemical messenger dopamine. In the brain a number of neurotransmitters connect one neuron to another. Among these neurotransmitters are dopamine and serotonin. New brain-imaging technologies made it possible to measure the extent of the inhibition of a particular transmitter. Thus, the neuroleptic (neuron-grabbing) drugs were shown to work by partially shutting down dopamine nerve pathways between neurons and thus inhibiting communication between them. By blocking dopamine reception, the communication system of the brain is inhibited at three levels: on the level of motor movement, on the level of emotional response, and on the level of cognition. The results are the symptoms of Parkinson's on the motor level, apathy and detachment on the emotional level, and mental dulling on the level of cognition.[26]

Once it was determined that Thorazine "worked" by inhibiting dopamine neurotransmitters, it was a short step to claiming that what "caused" mental illness was an excess of dopamine. In fact there has been no evidence that schizophrenics suffered from excess dopamine before receiving the drugs, but it did appear that inhibiting dopamine transmitters caused the brain to compensate by producing more dopamine transmitters. A rapid withdrawal from taking the neuroleptic drugs thus left the patient with an excess of dopamine, which then triggered a psychotic relapse. Thus, the question raised by neuroleptic drug critics, such as Robert Whitaker, is whether the drugs were actually inducing a problem rather than curing it.[27]

Nevertheless, the language quickly adopted as definitive by the advocates of the drugs was that the cause of schizophrenia is a "chemical imbalance in the brain," that is, an excess of dopamine, which is then remedied by inhibiting it. Since this excess is assumed to be a permanent impairment in the brain, this means that taking the medication to inhibit dopamine's role in brain communication is not seen as a short-term solution, but permanent, similar to the way that diabetics have to take insulin for the rest of their lives.[28]

The complexity of identifying excess dopamine as the "cause" of schizophrenia was summarized by research psychiatrist E. Fuller Torrey, himself committed to the brain disease theory of cause and drugs as the main solution:

> Despite the longevity and theoretical attractiveness of dopamine and other neurochemical theories, these theories also have several short-comings. Most research is carried out on postmortem brain specimens, and it is often difficult to know how much the chemicals have changed after death. It is also known that antipsychotic medication may affect many of these chemicals, and many initially promising findings have been shown later to have been a drug effect. The most important criticism of dopamine and other neurochemical theories of schizophrenia, however, is that they are not really theories of causation but rather theories of the pathophysiology or process of the disease. If altered dopamine *is* the cause, how did it become altered? Possible answers are genetic defect, stress, a virus, etc., but some other theory must be invoked to explain the altered dopamine.[29]

Once it had been ascertained that a brain disease was the cause of schizophrenia and drugs were the solution, medically trained psychiatrists became disinterested, if not hostile, to any kind of talk therapy. It was declared to be useless, if not counterproductive. In E. Fuller Torrey's words:

> There is some evidence that psychoanalysis and insight-oriented psychotherapy may not only be useless for treating schizophrenia, but may in fact be harmful. In the May study [A study by Philip R. A.

May at Camarillo State Hospital, California] for example, the "outcome for patients who received only psychotherapy was significantly worse than in the no-treatment control group." In other words, getting no treatment at all led to better outcomes than being treated by psychotherapy alone. This correlates with the individual experience of many psychotherapists who have given up treating such patients with insight-oriented psychotherapy because many of their patients seemed to get worse.[30]

Actually, the May study Torrey cited showed that those who did best were treated either with drugs alone or with psychotherapy plus drugs. But Torrey's comments suggested that "insight-oriented" psychotherapy should be wholly rejected.

The common practice of psychiatrists today who treat those with mental illness has been to meet them briefly to give a battery of tests and ascertain the diagnosis of which mental illness seems indicated, and then to prescribe a combination of psychotropic drugs plus anti-depressants and drugs designed to counter the side effects of other drugs. Thereafter, the psychiatrist sees the patients for fifteen minutes every two months to check on the patient's experience of the medication and represcribe it.

A recent article in the *Archives of General Psychiatry* showed that patients receiving psychotherapy have fallen from 44.4 percent in 1996–1997 to 28.9 percent in 2004–2005, and those who receive psychotherapy are the wealthy who can pay out of pocket. This decline of psychotherapy in preference for short visits solely for medication is seen as primarily due to insurance reimbursement policies. Reimbursement for a fifty-minute psychotherapy session is 40.9 percent lower than for a fifteen-minute medication-management visit. This trend also is impelled by the "aggressive marketing of psychotropic medications to psychiatrists and patients."[31] These practices allow such psychiatrists to treat dozens, if not hundreds, of patients, particularly in a public-health setting. Such psychiatrists typically know little of the total life experience of such patients. Clearly, brain chemistry and drugs have trumped any kind of work as soul guides for the contemporary psychiatrist.[32]

The Quest for the Schizophrenic Gene:
Mental Illness and Heredity

E. Fuller Torrey's quotation about possible causes of schizophrenic brain chemistry "imbalance" included a reference to "genetic" causes. The notion that mental illness is due to bad heredity has had a notorious history in American treatment of those with mental illness. In the nineteenth century and the first half of the twentieth, American views of "the insane" bore a strong element of racial-ethnic prejudice. In the 1840s blacks were widely believed to be incapable of the demands of freedom; free blacks were seen as prone to insanity. Senator John Calhoun, leader of the Southern slave states, seized on this view to argue for the benefits of slavery for blacks: "Here is the proof of the necessity of slavery. The African is incapable of self-care and sinks into lunacy under the burden of freedom. It is a mercy to give him the guardianship and protection from mental death."[33]

The 1880s into the 1930s saw a wide popularity of Social Darwinism in the United States. Social Darwinism appropriated the idea of the "survival of the fittest" to define the "fit" and the "unfit" in American society. The fit were the Anglo-Saxon elite, those who naturally rose to the top in the contest of life. The unfit were blacks and "colored," Asians, Mexicans, and the Irish. They also included the immigrants of southern and eastern Europe who were entering the United States in large numbers at the end of the nineteenth century. These "unfit" were believed to tend to lunacy and imbecility, as well as criminality, alcoholism, and sexual perversion. They also tended to breed like rabbits, passing on their undesirable traits to their offspring.

WASP elitist thinkers mourned what they saw as the "race suicide" of the white Anglo-Saxon Protestants (WASP), whom they saw as the true Americans. This race suicide was coming about because of the startling failure of this elite to breed in sufficient numbers. Particular blame was placed on WASP women who were restless for higher education and careers and hence were not having large families, and many not marrying at all. Too much democracy was also seen as allowing the unfit to survive, rather than dying out, which would be their natural fate if they had to compete on equal terms with the white Anglo-Saxon Protestants.[34]

In the atmosphere of this kind of thinking, eugenic views grew in popularity, funded especially by leaders among the new class of millionaire "robber barons," such as Andrew Carnegie, John D. Rockefeller, and John Harvey Kellogg of the cereal empire, and favored by presidents of elite Ivy League universities. But the popularity of eugenic thinking went far beyond this circle of the wealthy and was widely defused among white Americans. Eugenicists favored immigration laws excluding "Orientals" and non-whites, as well as Jews, and eastern and southern Europeans. California, the leader in anti-Oriental exclusion, had already passed the Chinese Exclusion Act in 1882, extending it in 1902 and 1903. In 1924 the United States passed a comprehensive immigration act that excluded all Asians from immigration and allowed limited quotas for eastern and southern Europeans, while favoring those from the British Isles and Germany.

Eugenicists also advocated laws forbidding "the mentally retarded" and "the insane" from marrying. Already in 1896 Connecticut passed a law barring persons with insanity from marrying, and many other states followed. By 1933 most of the forty-eight states had such laws, but obviously such laws did not prevent this group from reproducing. Studies of the marriage patterns of persons with mental illness have continually revealed that they actually have a low marriage and reproduction rate, largely because of their tendency to social withdrawal, confinement, and poverty. Yet, the eugenicists continued to be haunted by the specter of persons with mental illness and other "unfit" scattering many children throughout the land, doomed to carrying on the "defective germ plasma" of their parents. They believed the only way to definitively prevent this group from breeding was to segregate them and then to sterilize them.

Indiana was the first state to pass a compulsory sterilization law in 1907, followed by California and Washington in 1909. By 1939 thirty-three states had passed such laws.[35] Although "the insane" and "the mentally retarded" were the prime targets of these laws of sterilization, many state legislatures defined a broad list of those who should not reproduce. Iowa, in its 1913 bill, listed those in need of sterilization as "criminals, rapists, idiots, feeble-minded, imbeciles, lunatics, drunk-ards, drug fiends, epileptics, syphilitics, moral and sexual perverts and diseased and degenerate persons."[36] Under many state laws, the blind, the deaf, the physically deformed, and Native Americans, as well as African American women, were sterilized. Puerto Rico also had a ster-ilization law under which many Puerto Rican women were sterilized without their consent after childbirth.

Although some people challenged the constitutionality of these laws, they were broadly supported. In a 1937 *Fortune* magazine poll, 66 percent of those asked favored sterilizing "defectives." At least 65,000 Americans were sterilized under such laws from 1907 to the 1950s, more than a third of them patients in mental hospitals. The numbers were probably far higher, but because of poor efforts to keep records, particularly of those sterilized without their consent, it is impossible to determine the full number. It was also common to sterilize those in pris-ons. California led the nation with half of these sterilizations.[37] Although the purpose of these laws was explicitly eugenic, some doctors in mental hospitals construed sterilization as "therapeutic," recommending it for men as restoring their vigor, and for women as a way of protecting them from unwanted children.[38]

These laws of sterilizing the "unfit" were widely copied in Europe, especially in Germany, which cited the United States as its model in this effort. American eugenicists also supported the movement in Germany. In 1925 the Rockefeller Foundation gave $2.5 million to the Psychi-atric Institute in Munich and additional money to the Kaiser Wilhelm Institute for Anthropology, Human Genetics and Eugenics in Berlin for eugenic research in Germany.[39]

When Hitler came to power in 1933, a comprehensive sterilization bill, The Prevention of Hereditarily Diseased Offspring, was passed, and 375,000 Germans were sterilized between 1933 and 1939. In 1940 Nazi Germany turned to gassing the mentally ill, killing 70,000 men-tal patients over the next 18 months. But protests of families brought this movement to a halt, and in the fall of 1941 the gas chambers were moved to the new concentration camps where they were used to exter-minate Jews and other "undesirables."

Sterilization laws in the United States did not disappear in the light of the revelation of this Nazi history, although the racial basis of eugenics was no longer acceptable. Twenty-seven states still had such laws on their books in 1956. About 4,000 mentally ill patients in hospitals were sterilized in the 1950s. The last forced sterilization occurred in Oregon in 1981. Governors of several states, such as Virginia, Washington, and California, have since apologized for these programs, although no compensation was offered, citing the few remaining victims (and, of course, no offspring) and inadequate records.[40]

Clearly any new effort to ascertain the genetic component in mental illness must distance itself from any eugenic interests. Yet researchers interested in the genetic basis of mental illness continue to cite research done in the 1920s to 1940s in the United States and Germany that is rooted in eugenic biases.[41] New studies seeking to identify the environmental and genetic components of schizophrenia have been undertaken more recently. These studies seek to find out what proportion of families with one schizophrenic parent have one or more schizophrenic children, what proportion of families with two schizophrenic parents have children who are schizophrenic, and the number of schizophrenics who have aunts and uncles, grandparents, and other relatives who are schizophrenics. They have particularly focused on the study of twins— both fraternal and identical, twins raised together and twins raised apart, and those adopted versus those raised in their natal families.

These studies claim to show clear correlations of vulnerability to schizophrenia with heredity, while discounting particular family social environments as causative. Typical of these statistics are the following: with identical twins raised together, when one is schizophrenic, there is about a 48 percent chance that the other will be also. When identical twins are raised apart, this vulnerability remains the same, thus family environment is discounted as an influence. Siblings have about 9 percent chance of being schizophrenic if a brother or sister is schizophrenic, and there is no difference if the siblings are fraternal twins. Families with a schizophrenic parent have about a 13 percent likelihood of having a schizophrenic child. This increases to 46 percent if both parents are schizophrenic. The risk for nieces and nephews of an

afflicted person is 3 percent and for grandchildren 3.7 percent. There
is about a 1 to 1.5 percent risk of any person in the general human
population getting schizophrenia who has no known relatives who are
or were schizophrenic.[42] These studies thus conclude that while heredity is a factor, it is not determinative. Even an identical twin who has the
same genes as a schizophrenic sibling has less than 50 percent chance
of getting schizophrenia.

Alvin Pam, professor of psychiatry at Southwest Medical Center
in Dallas, Texas, has severely criticized these "pedigree" studies of the
inheritance of mental illness. From the 1880s through the 1940s, such
studies were deeply biased by racist and eugenic interests. More recent
studies have been biased by a biological reductionism that seeks to find
primarily genetic causes of psychological disorders. This, Pam believes,
results in very questionable research designs that systematically screen
out the social and environmental factors. Confident claims are based on
slight evidence; for example, identical twins "reared apart" when there
are hardly any cases of schizophrenic identical twins actually reared
apart in the sense of totally different family environments and without
any contact with each other. In Pam's view "a hereditary predisposition
to schizophrenia is (still) not a proven scientific fact."[43]

Some researchers believe that the vulnerability to schizophrenia
has been constant throughout history and in all cultures and social
classes, at about one in a hundred, although the data to prove this
constancy throughout history seems guess work, since there is little
data for the percentages of schizophrenics in earlier societies. Others believe the vulnerability has increased with modern civilization.
A World Health Organization study over eight years, starting in 1969,
showed that schizophrenia in urban Western societies is more severe
and those afflicted are less likely to recover than in simpler societies in
India and Africa.[44]

There is no proof that particular social classes are more likely to
become schizophrenic than others; those who are poor are no more
likely than those who are affluent, or vice versa, although the majority
of schizophrenics become poor because they fall out of the job market.
Vulnerability to schizophrenia is said to be widely dispersed throughout

the human population and probably involve many genes rather than just one. The conclusion of these studies is that some combination of genetic vulnerability plus some social stresses or traumas are causative, but neither genes nor any particular social stress has been shown to be determinative.

Since neither inheriting the same genes nor being raised in the same family is determinative, what "causes" schizophrenia seems to remain as unknown as ever. Why does one child in a family with a schizophrenic parent become schizophrenic, while there is an 87 percent chance that the other children of that same family will not? Why does one child with no known relatives with schizophrenia and a healthy, supportive family have a 1 percent chance of getting schizophrenia, while a child with a highly conflicting family and no relatives with mental illness has about the same likelihood of becoming schizophrenic? Our son David seems to belong to that 1 percent of the human population who becomes schizophrenic with no known relatives with schizophrenia, either close or distant. Although he had his share of "social stresses" growing up, they do not seem to have been particularly remarkable. (See his own reflections at the end of this chapter on "causes," where he attributed his "problems" primarily to taking "acid.")

This wide dispersal of the vulnerability to schizophrenia throughout the human population, with some evidence of a worsening incidence of it in modern urban societies, has led some researchers to speculate that the genes for schizophrenia are part of the general human condition. One of these researchers is British psychiatrist David Horrobin, author of *The Madness of Adam and Eve: How Schizophrenia Shaped Humanity*.[45] Horrobin argues that the genes for schizophrenia, also for dyslexia, bipolar disorder, and depression, appeared with mutations that transformed hominids into modern humans about 100,000 BC. This transformation of the brain took place before the migration of humans out of Africa and are thus a common heritage of all humans, found in the same percentages (about 1 percent) in all races and cultures in all social contexts, including Australian Aboriginals, who were separated from other human groups as long ago as 80,000 BC. The same genes that tend toward these mental illnesses and dysfunctions also underlie all kinds of musical, artistic, and intellectual creativity, but also the paranoid view of others as enemies and the need to dominate others. In short, the same brain mutations that made us human, with a capacity for imagination and creativity as well as domineering aggression, also made us prone to mental illness.

Although Horrobin believes that schizophrenia appears in all human groups in about the same percentage, its severity varies, with modern industrialized societies exhibiting the most severe and long-lasting expression of the illness and simple preindustrialized societies the mildest cases with better prognosis of recovery. Horrobin cites the World Health Organization study mentioned previously to support this view. He sees a link between the severity and duration of schizophrenia and the loss of essential fatty acids from the human diet. This began with the turn to grains as the basis of the human diet with the agricultural revolution (about 10,000 to 5,000 BC) and became more severe with the turn of industrialized societies to processed food in the nineteenth century.

Horrobin believes that a key cause of this increasing severity of schizophrenia is the loss of fatty acids, mainly from fish and other water-based animals. These fatty acids feed the membrane phospholipids (fatty tissues) of the brain that activate or slow down the neurotransmitters. It is this loss of fatty acids in these membranes, and not the excess of dopamine, that increases the severity of schizophrenia. Hence, a way of modifying this severity is to supplement the modern human diet with fish oil containing these essential fatty acids.

Horrobin and a team of researchers from several European countries tested regular supplements of fish oil in the diets of both schizophrenics and violent criminals and found a significant lessening of the symptoms of agitation and violence without the negative side effects of neuroleptics. Horrobin criticizes the promotion of the dopamine thesis. He sees the dopamine-inhibiting drugs as having little effect on the symptoms of schizophrenia for 75 to 85 percent of those afflicted, while causing severe side effects such as Parkinson's disease, permanent brain damage, facial and body tics (tardive dyskinesia), weight gain, and a general dumbing down of the person. Psychiatrists and the drug companies promoting these drugs have downplayed the severity of these side effects, while at the same time scorning relatively inexpensive dietary aids such as fish oils, which might be helpful.[46]

Intrigued by Horrobin's thesis, I sought the advice of a psychiatric researcher at UCLA and also a practicing psychiatrist working in a program sponsored by the Mental Health Association of Los Angeles. Both were unacquainted with Horrobin's work. The researcher angrily dismissed "dietary solutions" out of hand as worthless, while the practicing psychiatrist indicated his ignorance and disinterest in diet as a factor in schizophrenia. By contrast, Charles Barber, lecturer in psychiatry at the Yale University School of Medicine and author of the recent book *Comfortably Numb: How Psychiatry Is Medicating a Nation*, on the overuse of antidepressants in American society, sees various elements that help prevent children from developing schizophrenia and antisocial disorders. On diet he affirms that "fish oil, for example, appears to be very good stuff for the brain and behavior which makes sense because omega-3 fatty acids have a critical role in brain development and functioning, including promoting the growth of neurons in the frontal cortex."[47]

Barber cites studies by Andrew Stoll at Harvard that indicate fish oil eases the symptoms of bipolar disorder and depression; he also refers to studies by Bernard Gesch of the University of Oxford, where prisoners fed a diet rich in fish showed a marked reduction of assaults and other disciplinary violations.[48]

Toward a Holistic Theory of Mind-Brain Interaction

The current language about brain chemistry as the "cause" of schizophrenia seems to assume a somewhat mechanical view of the brain and body in which a disorder of the brain chemistry of unknown cause is remedied by chemical agents that counter this disorder, that is, excess dopamine corrected by dopamine inhibitors. What this view fails to reckon with is a dynamically organic understanding of the relation of the mental and the somatic in which thought and experience constantly interact with and change brain chemistry. Several issues point to a need for greater awareness of mind-brain interaction. One of these is the question of why schizophrenia tends to develop in late adolescence. A 2003 study by two researchers from the School of Psychology of the University of Birmingham in England, Chris Harrop and Peter Trower, examines this question with what they call a "cognitive-developmental approach."[49]

Adolescence is recognized to be a crucial time in human development when the brain is reorganizing itself and undergoing a vast process of synaptic pruning; the other two times this happens are in infancy and old age. Adolescence is also a time of critical personal-social transition when the young person negotiates the basic changes of social status from being a child dependent on parents to an independent person, creating a sense of the self that is both personally satisfactory and confirmed by peers. It is not accidental that in the evangelical Christian tradition late adolescence has also been the typical period when a person falls into a deep emotional depression and concern over his or her sinfulness, which is to be resolved by a conversion experience (see chapter 2).

What Harrop and Trower point to as a largely ignored phenomenon in schizophrenic research is that many of the patterns of thought and behavior of adolescence mirror that of psychosis. The key changes of social status typically involve authority conflicts as the adolescence struggles to define greater independence from parents. The adolescent needs to deidealize parents and other authority figures and recognize them as fallible older peers. Adolescents going through this period often exhibit expressions of depression and fears of worthlessness, together with egocentricity, grandiosity, and a sense that one is the center of the universe. They also seek new mentors and ideals as childhood mentors are dethroned. Loneliness, depression, delusionlike fantasy, and beliefs that what one thinks is the same as what others are thinking often characterize adolescence. These problems seem more acute in males, which may be related to the way in which society presents males with more grandiose ideals of what they are supposed to achieve and become in society.

Harrop and Trower see adolescent psychotic breakdown as cases where this turmoil becomes more acute and people become "stuck" in the transition between a childhood self dependent on parents and an adult person who has successfully negotiated an independent self. This means a self that is realistic in its understanding of who one is in relation to others, neither setting up a grandiose self that is not acknowledged by others nor being sunk in a sense of worthlessness. Although psychotropic drugs can have a role in alleviating symptoms, for Harrop and Trower the key to moving beyond this schizophrenic breakdown is cognitive-behavioral therapy in which the mentally disturbed person develops the realistic self and relation to others that had become blocked.

For Harrop and Trower an important component of rethinking schizophrenia as blocked adolescent development is to reconceive the mind-brain relationship:

> The first alternative that we propose is that *many* (or perhaps *most* or even *all*) *of the biological differences seen in the brains of people suffering from psychosis are produced by the psychotic symptoms.* Thus biological differences would be a biological response to or implementation of a psychotic mental state. This changes the direction of causality round so that the symptoms of psychosis can be viewed on a par with the biological in determining the cause of the condition. . . .
>
> Another more satisfactory proposal is: *the biological and psychological work in a reciprocal and iterative fashion* . . . symptoms produce changes in the brain and . . . these in turn shape the form of the symptoms. These would be not discrete actions but ongoing and reciprocal interchanges. [50]

One well-known example of severe environmental stress causing changes in brain chemistry, which is expressed in ongoing psychosis, is posttraumatic stress disorder (PTSD), a phenomenon known in earlier wars by other names, such as "shellshock" in World War I. PTSD as a category of mental illness was included in the "psychiatric Bible" of mental disorders, the *DSM*, only after Vietnam veterans lobbied to have it included in the 1970s in order to make the federal government cover the medical costs for this condition.[51]

PTSD is a severe anxiety disorder that can develop after exposure to terrifying events that threaten or cause severe physical harm to oneself or others. People with PTSD display pathological changes in neurological wiring created by extreme fear. There is debate about the exact neurobiology of PTSD and also whether those who experience it already have a predisposition to it, either due to genes or previous experiences of trauma. But experiences of extreme stress clearly are the immediate occasion of a psychosis expressed in ongoing flashbacks, phobias, violent outbursts, and other symptoms.[52]

Although war-related trauma is the best-known source of PTSD today, with one in five servicemen and -women returning from the wars in Iraq and Afghanistan since 2002 suffering from PTSD, other traumatic and life-threatening events are also known to cause it. The *DSM-IV-TR* lists many kinds of violent personal assault, including sexual assault, robbery, mugging, being kidnapped or taken hostage, natural and manmade disasters, automobile accidents, terrorist attack, and being tortured. After PTSD became a diagnostic category in the *DSM*, more attention was given to sexual assault or abuse as one cause of PTSD.[53]

It is significant that the Freudian psychoanalytic tradition failed to address sexual abuse as a cause of psychosis. Instead, Freud repressed and misinterpreted the evidence that many of the women with psychotic symptoms who came to him for help had suffered sexual abuse in the family. Initially Freud believed them, but when he was heavily criticized for accepting the women's accounts and after hearing a patient report that a personal friend of Freud's was a sexual abuser, he changed his views and decided that the women were fantasizing about their sexual abuse.[54]

This interpretation of the women's stories of sexual abuse became a key part of his theory that female children desired sexual relations with their fathers and their psychosis came from repression of these desires (Electra complex). For many feminist critics of Freud, women thus became doubly abused in Freudian theory, both denying the reality of their sexual abuse and then blaming them as fantasizing these memories as their own sexual desires, the denial of which caused their psychosis.

A great deal of new research from 1996 to the present has emphasized the plasticity of the brain and the reciprocal interaction of mind and brain, environmental learning, and changes in brain chemistry and neurological pathways. Some of this work was pioneered by psychiatrist Eric Kandel, a Viennese Jew who, with his family, fled the Nazis in 1939. The issue of memory fascinated Kandel: How do traumatic experiences, such as the knock on the door of his family's apartment by Nazis in 1939, become imprinted in the brain, to be vividly recalled many years later?[55]

Kandel's training in both psychoanalysis and neuroscience led him to ask how learning changes the brain. To answer this question he turned to one of the simplest animals, the Aplysia, a large sea snail whose brain contains only 20,000 cells (compared with 100 billion in mammals), but is large enough to be observed with the naked eye. By prodding the snail in the gills and shocking it on its head or tail, Kandel was able to show that brain cells changed as the animal learned to avoid the shocks or became hypersensitive to them. He found that the synapses between neurons could easily and systematically change in response to stimulation: "In Aplysia, you can see before your eyes that the connections change. When an animal remembers something for the long term, it grows new synaptic connections."[56]

In his pioneering article, "A New Intellectual Framework for Psychiatry,"[57] Kandel laid out the interactive relation of environmental experience and brain chemistry. Columbia University neuroscientist Norman Doidge writes: "Kandel's work demonstrates that the common metaphor that compared the mind to a computer, with unmodifiable hardware (the brain) and malleable software (thoughts, memories) is wrong. Rather thoughts can actually change the structure of the brain, the software modifies the hardware."[58]

Genetic theory is also becoming less mechanistic, recognizing that experience can modify how genes behave and these modifications can be inherited by offspring. Environmental factors, such as diet and stressful experiences, have biological effects that determine how genetic traits are actually activated. This is recognized in many animals, such as honeybees. All female honeybees come from genetically identical larvae, but those fed on royal jelly become fertile queens, while the others become sterile workers. This new recognition of how experience changes the way genes actually work could have important consequences for understanding how diseases are inherited, including schizophrenia, bipolar disorder, cancer, and diabetes.[59]

This understanding of the interaction of learning and brain chemistry means psychiatry must go beyond the false dichotomies: mind versus brain, environment versus genes, psychotherapy versus medication, soul guides versus scientists, the social versus the biological.[60] The long war between psychosocial and biological views of mental illness needs to be overcome in a genuinely biopsychosocial view.[61] All of these aspects need to be seen in their complex interaction. For example, forms of psychotherapy that retrain cognition and behavior may be able to change the neurons that support destructive patterns of thought and behavior more effectively and more long term than medications whose workings are not fully known. In Kandel's view, psychology and neuroscience need to mutually inform each other, "interactively and synergistically, not only additively."[62]

David's Reflections on Causes

To conclude this chapter on the causes of schizophrenia, I include a reflective piece written by David in his diary on December 17, 1982, when he was twenty-three years old. He was then in the early years of his illness. He speculates on the causes of his sickness:

> *Did not go to Thresholds today* [the psychiatric program he had been attending] *and have been thinking about my sickness (dreams last night of making the corner of our house into a curve and of breathing hard in a state of unsurety whether I was asleep or awake, then had a hard time getting up and too tired for Thresholds). My question is when did the sickness really start?* Nelsons [a friend's family]? *Gonzaga* [his high school]? *Chris Warner* [a close friend]? *Oliver* [his sister's boyfriend]? *Mr. Baker* [a neighbor]? *Cambridge* [his school in Cambridge, England]? *And what is the reality behind said sickness when all defenses are dropped? (acid? girls? Medication? Failures in school? Social life, such as Drama Society?)*
>
> *I think that acid and something about my personal delusions are responsible, especially acid in that the "revolving door" is so dangerous and deceptive. But there must be something else, such as a physical problem or imbalance which was at one time a symptom of the*

drug scene and personal delusions, and then aggravated by Medication. This must be a serious thing which I am not the only casualty of, though I refuse to believe that my physical shortcomings are so much different from others, and also from a kind of mystical and spiritual body problems. Yet marijuana makes one feel better and so does beer, and there is a difference between questioning reality and having no reality (Medication), which is a difference which also entails a significant aspect of living in these modern times. Also some ways that I see as relevant to my problems are evident, that some people make a living off "my" problems, and, of course, these types of mind were important to me in high school.

But, as for my problems, I have to say that I don't know, except that it is frustrating and has no bearing on my "thinking." Also I know that my thinking is the only thing that pulls me through at times. The only other thing I'm sure of is that physically I have limitations, so that my parents have the right to give me Meds. in a sense, but only in that I can only go so long being myself (without social life, etc, etc) without becoming somewhat suicidal. But the easy answer for me is nothing more than a night out with Oliver or Hamp [a friend] and maybe a few beers or bowls and then no more suicide. So really it is a question of time. So too bad that never happens . . .

So I can only attribute my problems to no social life, time and a confusing juxtaposition of myself as a loner and as a person who has more to give with each other. So that the result is a person who has gone through a maze of so-called "help" (Meds.) when what he needed was a cause to help with. And finally the simple fact that I can give only when I'm allowed space for having my own thoughts, which means that my problem might be a symptom of society and the mental health system and/or an individual who does not understand how to live without objecting to the forces of death.

My problem then being that something I feel deathlike is either present or non-existent, as I can tell that I am happy or sad, dead or alive, good or bad, pretty or ugly, "full" or empty. And I am only sure of something so far: my objection is not to myself. It is to "others," yet I know my problem is real, so I have to look deeper at everything, since I find the world so simple, and say: "Why should I live the way the world is made?" If the world is simple and I am sick, so that life must be cruel, then I want to be able to make my own world. It is irrelevant whether "the world" is handed to me on a silver platter, because I don't want it. I want to make my own world and survive that way in order to find out my limitations more truthfully. And if I am too sick for that, tell me why I'm writing this, instead of fighting to survive?

In ending I can genuinely say that although I admit to being sick, I can also find many other factors which are no fault of mine, such as the dearth of other choices for myself in life, so that I am forced to be at the whim of powers which should not be necessary for me. In other words, my lack of choices makes me sick because of the great pain I am forced to bear in a world which does not belong to me, so that I am helpless to do anything for myself. In other words, the world is my enemy now, as I am unable to use the world in any way due to the way people have built a world where I am only moving around myself, instead of moving around a great world of nature and life.

Many of David's poems in this period reflect a mood bordering on existential despair, feeling in the grip of death and yet seeking to fight through to a more life-giving world. This theme of death as the underlying reality was prominent in his adolescent writings even before the onset of schizophrenia. This mood is reflected in this poem:

"The Sprig"

The sprig of young growth
The newborn tree of the Spring
The small sprig that will barely survive
The winter freeze.
It is now the autumn's gull
Lulled by an easy birth
And a lazy summer
Into the autumn of its youthful innocence.
It will soon find out it has been gulled.
The frost will bite its tiny twigs.
The wind will burn it with pain
And the dark nights will bring death.
The snow will seem a gift from heaven,
If it survives.
And when the shock is lifted,
And the sun showers down on its smallest angel,
The baby sprig will spit outs its vengeance,

Thrashing wildly to be free of this cold, black hell.
Then when the tide has passed and the storm abides,
The sprig will fight its way up to heaven
Until it reaches the rooftops
And has spread its little fingers
In every direction,
To be with the mother sun's warm embrace.

David's 1982–1983 diary contains several love poems that seem to be written more to a female alter ego than a particular person. One of these, "Making a Friend of a Mannequin," expresses a poignant sense of life in the grip of death:

"Making a Friend of a Mannequin"

I danced with her in a cathedral ballroom
With the saints and the walls
Gathering us into the halls of the past.
Where the life we lacked
Was made up by the grave mask
We both wore in the castle of God.

She was so pale and death was in her.
Blank stares at me,
But I loved her until the end
And I call her my only friend.
I know she has a heart,
Though I guessed she wasn't mine,
But since we were together anyway,
She was my best friend
For the night we would spend.
So lovely in the dungeon,
Smoking our tears
And drinking our dear prayers.

Please give us back an answer.
She only needs her one dream
For the two of us to find the means
For once to be our real Jesus Christ
And one and all to be so free.

Please feel for me
And feel some sympathy
For the life-sized doll
Who can never see.
She's smoking her tears,
Drinking her prayers
To Jesus Christ,
Swimming stationary
In the coldest sink,
Praying alone and fighting back.
The dreaming sorrow
Which keeps her hollow
The naked dear of an unclothed here.

Just give me her anyway
I know she has nothing
And she can't talk
Or tell me how she feels
But I want her all to myself.
I can make her look so beautiful
And she will always stay young
While I become the old man
Who will one day join her
In the world of lost love
Which the people of the world
Will only call death.
Looking down at the bottom
Of the blackest hole
In the farthest door
Of the dark black earth,
Facing the cold and fire,
Breaking my balls
And changing into a dead zombie.
She is waiting for me there
Where I lie on the stone shelf
In the house of love.

And when I go away
And climb the stairs
Or fall down the spiraling trap,

I will carry her with me,
The two of us fusing into one.
Whatever will come
In the bleak house
Where all must go
To find the wild goose
We have been chasing.
But she will be with me
And I will know
She is only a life-sized model.

Deranged and hell-fired,
Walking the black pits
I keep her from the fire
And sleep with her
So close to the gates of hell
Where she could leave
If only she had a soul.
But, again, it is the same problem,
She has a body,
I have a soul
But both are lost somehow now
In the dirt and the mines.

One day we will escape,
When I have bought her a soul
From a long dead inmate.
Then we will share her body together,
Going along with each other
Everywhere we have longed for.

Treating Persons with Mental Illness

Why Such Poor Treatment?

Why have people with mental illness been "treated" so badly in the history of their "care" in western Europe and the United States? To explore this question, we have to approach the feelings and cultural views of mental illness in our societies, that is, our attitudes toward people with mental illness and how this has conditioned how we treat them. "Treatment" here means both various kinds of measures claimed as "medical" to try to "cure" or "calm" those with mental illness and general ways of dealing with and responding to them in culture and society.

Overcoming Our Fear of Mental Illness

One of the problems we run up against is the perception of people with mental illness as dangerously violent. The National Alliance on Mental Illness (NAMI) has been engaged in campaigns to overcome stigma toward this population.[1] They want particularly to combat the impression that those with mental illness are irrationally violent and are the ones primarily involved in public massacres, such as the one that occurred at Virginia Polytechnic in April 2007. This campaign against stigma seeks to inform Americans that the number of people with mental illness, particularly schizophrenics and manic depressives, who are violent is very small in number and that most of them are not violent. Thus one press release in response to the media coverage of the massacre at Virginia Polytechnic states: "The U.S. Surgeon General has reported that the likelihood of violence by people with mental illness is low. In fact, 'the overall contribution of mental disorders to the total level of violence in society is exceptionally small.' More often, people living with mental illness are victims of violence."[2]

While the information put out by this NAMI campaign is accurate enough, it evades the most difficult aspect of the problem. When those with mental illness are violent, much of this violence is directed at their own families. A person with mental illness is far more likely to injure a family member than to be involved in public violence. It is precisely this kind of violence that is so terrifying. Those of us who have had a schizophrenic family member living with the family know the terror of having him (or her) suddenly go into a rage, kick down the door of the bedroom, or start breaking china and furniture in the home. It is the unpredictability of such violence, and the losing of the safety of one's home, that is particularly frightening.

But the phobia toward people with mental illness is wider and more ambiguous than simply fear of their potential violence. I suspect it has to do with the fragility of rationality and our uncertainty about what is real. Surrounded as we are by various competing claims about what is real and what is not, with public figures telling us one minute that we must launch a major war in Iraq to defend ourselves against "weapons of mass destruction" and finding out the next minute that these did not exist; with some religious leaders shouting that homosexual marriage will be "the end of Western civilization," while others support it as an extension of human rights; with uncertainty about whether our food is contaminated and whether we are being poisoned by our air and water, it is no wonder that people cling to small touchstones of certainty and security, such as "God and guns," as the then Democratic presidential candidate Barack Obama put it.

Many have suggested that this fear of the "crazy" has greatly increased in modern secular societies that are supposedly based on rationality and science. More traditional societies, based on a faith that God or the gods had determined the patterns of the universe, seem to have been more tolerant of the "shatter-headed" as a part of their community. Post-Enlightenment Western societies, by contrast, have a greater need to pin down the parameters of the rational and to clearly separate out the irrational. Thus, the urgent need to separate the "mad" from "normal" society, to gather them in separate asylums where they could be "treated" and clearly differentiated from the "rest of us," which alarmingly seemed to lead to the multiplication of those seen as needing to be segregated. The struggle to keep the "normal" in control of a defined realm of sanity led to more strenuous efforts to build more and more asylums to segregate the "crazy." This project was paralleled by desperate efforts to keep "degenerates" from migrating to these shores, while preventing those already present in our society from reproducing.

For many people, what is unsettling is to realize that the borders between madness and sanity are variably permeable, that there are elements of insanity in all of us, and that it is not easy to be sure where one ends and the other begins. One response to this uncertainty is the expanding medicating of American society. More and more people, including small children, are put on antidepressants and other such medications. Problems traditionally seen as part of human finitude and fallibility are defined as mental illnesses to be dealt with by medication. There is a loss of the traditions of soul nurture that allowed people to accept their finitude and fallibility as "forgiven," as not separating them from ultimate reality.[3]

Chains and Other Restraints to Control the Unruly

"Restraints" refers to various ways in which mental hospitals, asylums, and poorhouses over the years have immobilized the bodies of people with mental illness in order to prevent them from acting out in ways seen as dangerous or annoying to the staff of the facility, such as injuring others or themselves, throwing or breaking things, or simply yelling and thrashing about. The history of restaints has shown that they have been used primarily for the convenience of the staff, other patients, and the institution, rather than as anything that was of help to the ill person, although it often has been claimed to be a way of "calming" them.

The most common form of restraint used in mental hospitals during the seventeenth to nineteenth centuries was chains. The person with mental illness was chained to the wall or the floor of his or her cell. Sometimes this chaining was extensive and left on for years. The American sailor James Norris was committed to the Bethlehem Hospital for the Insane (referred to as "bedlam") in 1800. There in a small cell he was chained by the feet to his bed. An iron harness riveted to an upright bar bound him sitting up, allowing him almost no movement even to lie down. After spending fourteen years in this condition he was discovered in 1814 by reformers and released, only to die soon after.[4]

In mental hospitals in the early nineteenth century, it was common for the cells for the "insane" to be in the basement, damp and without heat, with only straw for beds. It was frequently claimed that the "insane" were impervious to cold, pain, and hunger, and thus it was unnecessary to give them adequate food, heat, or even clothing. Neglect and filthy surroundings were common. A visitor to Pennsylvania Hospital in the early nineteenth century reported:

> We next took a view of the Maniacs. Their cells are in the lower story, which is partly underground. Their cells are about ten feet square, made strong as a prison. . . . Here are both men and women, between twenty and thirty in number. Some of them have beds; most of them clean straw. Some of them are fierce and raving. Nearly or quite naked; some singing and dancing; some in despair; some were dumb and would not open their mouths.[5]

Viewing the "maniacs" was seen as an entertaining public spectacle in the United States, as well as in Europe. Townspeople would visit an insane asylum as a Sunday outing, taunting the chained patients to provoke them into a rage. Pennsylvania Hospital made some profit out of this curiosity by charging a four-pence fee.[6] This was also the custom at Bethlehem Hospital in London, an institution that goes back to medieval times.[7]

It was common in this period to see people with mental illness as similar to wild beasts who, having lost their reason, had lost what made them distinctively human. Not just chains but frequent beatings were seen as necessary to break their "will" and force them to submit to authority. Thomas Willis, one of the earliest English writers on insanity, reported in a 1684 volume, revealingly called *The Practice of Physick: Two Discourses Concerning the Souls of Brutes*:

> Discipline, threats, fetters and blows are needed as much as medical treatment. . . . Truly nothing is more necessary and more effective for the recovery of these people than forcing them to respect and fear intimidation. By this method, the mind, held back by restraint, is induced to give up its arrogance and wild ideas and it soon becomes meek and orderly. This is why maniacs often recover much sooner if they are treated with tortures and torments in a hovel instead of with medicaments.[8]

English "mad doctors" of the late eighteenth century had an arsenal of cures that involved purging, bleeding, blistering of the skin, and restraints. Some of these derived from theories of "balancing" the four humors of the body, but they also came from the belief that restoration to sanity involved breaking the "will" of patients and forcing them to submit to authority. These practices were applied even to King George III when he fell into a state of delirium in December 1788. The prominent London physician Francis Willis, who claimed he had cured "nine out of ten patients" in his private "mad-house," took control of the king, forcing him into a "strait-waistcoat" and, when he complained, into a restraining chair. The king was bled with leeches on his temples and blistered on his legs until they became infected, his food was laced with emetics to make him vomit, and he was sedated with opium. Remarkably, the king recovered in February, but whether these measures contributed to this recovery is questionable.[9]

More recent research has suggested that the king suffered from porphyria, a rare genetic disorder that can create high levels of toxic substances in the body causing temporary delirium.[10] He suffered two more brief breakdowns of mind and body, in 1801 and 1804, and then a final one in 1810–1820, when he sank into senility, deafness, and blindness.[11] The king's bouts of illness and delirium brought attention to and sympathy for people with mental illness in England, who previously had been treated with chains and whips. There began a new era of building mental hospitals for this group, including those who were "paupers." A new faith developed that mental illness might be "cured" with humane care and medical attention.[12]

The reformers of the late eighteenth and early nineteenth centuries in England, France, and the United States made a point of striking off the chains of those with mental illness and insisting on humane treatment. Benjamin Rush, a pioneering American doctor who was the head physician at Pennsylvania Hospital from 1783 to 1813, was both an abolitionist and an advocate of prison reform. He came to Pennsylvania Hospital determined to make it a model of humane treatment. The "insane" were moved into a new wing of the hospital where they could enjoy real beds with mattresses, opportunities to stroll around the ground, useful work such as gardening, and games and music.

Yet Rush also viewed those with mental illness alternatively as mad animals or as those who had regressed to undisciplined childhood who needed to be intimidated and forced to submit to authority. Thus, Rush invented various kinds of restraints that were intended to be more enlightened forms of "calming" the insane. One of these was the "tranquilizing chair," in which the patient sat upright with bound hands and feet and a strap across the chest. A box stuffed with linen covered the patient's head, with a small opening at the front that forced him or her to look straight ahead. A bucket for waste was placed under the seat of the chair, and the person might be forced to sit there for many hours, urinating and defecating in place.[13] It is hard to imagine what kind of "tranquilizing" took place after many hours in such a chair—perhaps reduction to a catatonic state!

American hospitals in the nineteenth century employed a variety of "restraints." There was the straitjacket, which bound the person's arms around the body, and muffs to confine the hands. There were straps to tie a person to his or her bed by both arms and legs and around the chest.[14] More ingenious devices for restraining the patients were also devised, such as the Utica crib, invented by French physician Aubanel in 1845 and adopted by the New York State Lunatic Asylum. This consisted of a box the length and width of a human body and about two feet high, with slats or screening on the sides and the lid. The person confined in such as bed was immobilized; unable to turn over, the patient most likely felt suffocated confined to such a small space. Again, one has to ask what kind of "calming" took place by being locked in such a "crib."[15]

In the nineteenth century a debate took place between British and American "mad doctors" on the use of such restraints in mental hospitals. The British, led by John Connolly of the Hanwell Asylum near London, abandoned such physical restraints in favor of putting the person in seclusion or administering a sedative.[16] American doctors insisted on the continuing need of restraints to prevent self-injury, injury to others, or "filthy habits," such as masturbation.[17]

In the 1970s Elyn Saks, professor at the University of Southern California Law School and writer on the legal rights of those with mental illness, experienced several psychotic episodes and was hospitalized in Oxford. Later, when she attended Yale Law School and again experienced some mental breakdown, she was exposed to American mental hospitals. She was horrified to find herself put into "restraints," strapped to her bed, a treatment that has been banned in British hospitals for two centuries.[18] In her volume on the rights of those with mental illness, Saks included a chapter on "Mechanical Restraints: Loosening the Bonds."[19] Saks concluded from her own experience, as well as from many other case studies, that restraints should not be used except briefly when there is real risk of injury to others and then only the least restrictive alternative should be sought.

Saks prefers the use of a seclusion room and tranquilizing medication to tying the person down. Strapping a person to a bed in "six point restraints" (spread eagle, with wrists and ankles secured and torso immobilized; the typical current type of restraint in use in the United States), the person is unable to move. Such restraints are an assault on the person's dignity. Even animals are never tied down so they cannot move at all. This places the person in a condition of total helplessness.

Moreover, despite the claim of preventing the person from injuring himself or herself, such restraints can be harmful. They cause deep aches and pains after a few hours, circulatory problems can result if the straps are tied too tightly, and they can cause death from choking or heart attack. Saks cites studies showing fifty to 150 deaths a year resulting from the use of restraints.[20]

Often, patients are left in such restraints for many hours, even off and on for years. The effect of such treatment is not "calming," but creates a sense of humiliation and degradation. The feeling of being rendered helpless can be terrifying. Although a patient may learn to avoid the behavior that caused such restraints, the overall therapeutic results are counterproductive. Rather, the person feels emotionally scarred by the experience and may seek some other way of retaliating. In short, restraints are not a way of actually helping the patient develop any inner self-knowledge or discipline

David experienced the use of restraints in several of the hospitals where he was committed, both in Illinois and in California. The following is a conversation we had on June 17, 2008, on his experience of "restraints."

RR: *"You experienced being put in restraints several times?"*

David: *"Yeah, in Illinois and in California."*

RR: *"What do they do, exactly?"*

David: *"They tie you to the bed by your wrists and by your ankles; you are lying on your back spread out."*

RR: *"How long do they keep you in restraints?"*

David: *"In ISPI* [Illinois State Psychiatric Institute] *they kept me in restraints all night long. At Hawthorne* [Los Angeles Metropolitan] *they are friendlier. It is usually about an hour."*

RR: *"What happened to cause them to do that?"*

David: *"Well, the first time I was having a bad reaction to the medication and I was trying to get help. I pushed my way into the nurse's station and shoved this one guy, and so they put me in restraints. Another time this one guy was saying bad things about you. I told him he was a jerk and to stop saying those things, and then I punched him, so they put me in restraints. I was very upset afterward and was walking up and down the corridor in a very disturbed state of mind. That was in Illinois. I don't remember what happened at Hawthorne."*

RR: *"So, did you find being put in restraints at all helpful?"*

David: *"No, not at all."*

Shock Treatments

"Mad doctors" in the late eighteenth to the first half of the twentieth centuries developed a variety of somatic interventions designed to shock patients "into their senses." Among these were several types of "hydrotherapy." Far from being calming, water was used in ways that shocked and terrified and even simulated drowning, in ways reminiscent of "water-boarding" torture used recently in military interrogations. Buckets of water were poured suddenly on the patient's head from a great height, or needlelike jets of water pummeled the body. In the "bath of surprise," a blindfolded patient was dropped suddenly into a cold bath through a trapdoor. Various methods of near drowning were devised, such as putting the patient into a box with holes drilled into it and lowering it into water or locking him or her into an iron cage and lowering it into a pond. Before the patient succumbed to drowning, the device was raised and he or she was revived. One wonders how many died in the process.[21]

Methods of using water to "treat" patients were developed in new forms in the first half of the twentieth century. One method was the prolonged bath with the patient strapped into a hammock in the bathtub and the top covered with a canvas sheet with a hole for the head. The tub was filled alternatively with cold and hot water and the patient's head wrapped in bandages to cut out other sensations. Patients were kept in this "water jacket" for hours and even days on end. Another method was the wet pack, with sheets dipped in cold or hot water and wrapped tightly around the patient with an outer rubber sheet and a blanket, and then the patient was tied to the bed so they could not move. As the sheets dried, they tightened around the patient, giving a sensation of suffocation.[22]

Although doctors saw these baths and wet packs as therapeutic, conjecturing that they drained toxins from the body, patients often saw little difference between them and the older kind of restraints, such as straitjackets or being tied to the bed with straps.[23] As Joel Braslow has argued in his *Mental Ills and Bodily Cures*, doctors tended to define the nature of the disease according to the "cures" selected, failing to differentiate between control and cure, or to distinguish what was convenient for the institution from what actually helped the patient. If being noisy and hostile was defined as the manifestation of the mental illness, then whatever made patients "quiet" was regarded as therapeutic or curative.[24]

In the nineteenth century spinning the patient rapidly first in one direction and then the other was seen as a way of creating dizziness and terror. Englishman Joseph Cox invented a spinning chair that induced extreme vertigo, together with vomiting and emptying of the bladder and bowels.[25] American physician Benjamin Rush, inventor of the tranquilizing chair, also developed a spinning board, to which the patient was strapped and spun around rapidly. Rush believed that madness was caused by poor blood circulation and could be improved both by bleeding and by being spun on this "gyrator" board.[26]

In the first half of the twentieth century, various chemical methods of inducing a coma were introduced and were widely used, including malarial fever therapy, Metrazol convulsive therapy, insulin shock therapy, as well as electroconvulsive therapy.

Malarial fever therapy was developed by Austrian psychiatrist Julius Wagner-Jauregg after he noticed that some psychotic patients improved after a bout of fever. During World War I he took blood from a soldier with malaria and injected it into a patient suffering paresis (paralysis) caused by syphilis. The patient suffered nine attacks of malaria fever, and gradually recovered, overcoming paresis in the process. Wagner-Jauregg claimed he then experimented with nine (ten?) other patients, three of whom went home alive and were still well after a year, three who improved initially and then worsened, two who were unchanged, one who developed severe "paralytic melancholy," and one who died of the fever. Wagner-Jauregg published his results, claiming a six-out-of-nine success rate. In 1928 he received the Nobel Prize in medicine.[27]

Fever therapy became the rage for some years until the development of penicillin in the mid-1940s put an end to its use.[28] Fever therapy seems to have been helpful with paresis known to be caused by a particular infection. The high fever apparently killed or slowed the spirochete from the syphilis. Whether it helped any other kind of psychosis is questionable.[29] Based on his studies of the use of fever therapy in California mental hospitals, Joel Braslow commented on the changed doctor-patient relationship created by the new medical intervention. When tertiary-stage syphilis was seen as hopeless, doctors tended to disdain the patients as "degenerates" receiving their just punishment for an immoral life. Once there was a medical intervention that could actually alleviate the illness, doctors became more interactive with patients, consulting them on their wishes.[30]

Metrazol convulsive therapy consisted of inducing seizures by administrating camphor (later Metrazol, a synthetic camphor) to schizophrenics to counteract their psychosis. It was first tried by Hungarian doctor Ladislas Meduna in 1935. The Metrazol triggered such violent convulsions that it could fracture bones, loosen teeth, and tear muscles, as well as cause hemorrhages of internal organs. The experience was so terrifying that patients vehemently resisted it, even though the doctors believed it worked only when administered twenty to forty times, two or three times a week. The result was an initial tractability where patients were reduced to a childlike state, but they soon manifested their former psychosis. Thus, whether anyone was improved by it depends on what one calls "improvement." It was used by about 70 percent of American hospitals by 1939, with 37,000 patients receiving it between 1936 and 1941.[31] It was superseded by insulin shock therapy, which was seen as easier to control.

Insulin therapy was first developed by Viennese psychiatrist Manfred Sakel in 1933. It consisted of giving patients massive amounts of insulin to cause convulsions followed by a coma. After the person was comatose for some hours, glucose was administered to wake the person up. This too was administered twenty to forty times in succession. This therapy took a great deal of intensive care by physicians and nurses to be sure that the glucose was administered before the coma became fatal. Although very high rates of cures were claimed, 70 to 90 percent, these claims become dubious on more careful study. One to two percent died from complications, such as hypoglycemic brain damage, heart failure, and cerebral hemorrhage.[32] Many who were released as cured did not fare well in society and soon returned to the hospital. Yet, it remained a common treatment for schizophrenia in U.S. hospitals into the mid-1950s, despite reports that it did more harm than good. It resulted in making the patients passive and childlike, sleeping most of the time, and it seems to have done actual brain damage, destroying nerve tissue in the cortex.[33]

Of these various kinds of fever and shock therapies popular in the 1930s to 1950s, only one continues to be used. This is electroconvulsive therapy. Electroshock was developed by Italian psychiatrist Ugo Cerletti in 1938 after observing the use of electroshock to stun pigs in a slaughterhouse. It was introduced into American hospitals in 1940 and was widely used in the 1940s and 1950s. There was some decline in its use after severe criticism in the 1960s and 1970s, but it still continues to be used commonly today.[34] About 100,000 people were receiving ECT in the United States in the 1980s and about a million annually worldwide.[35]

Electroshock is usually administered by first giving a muscle relaxant and an anesthetic to prevent such violent convulsions that bones are broken. Electrodes are then put on either side of the patient's head (bilateral ECT) or on one side (unilateral ECT), and an electric pulse is sent through the cortex, inducing a severe seizure and loss of consciousness. Usually there is a course of six to twelve treatments two or three times a week, although at its high point of use in the 1940s to 1950s, patients could receive it hundreds of times. How it actually worked has never been clear, with practice tending to generate theory. Thus, the California Biennial Report for 1950–1952 of the Department of Mental Hygiene contains this vague statement: "The exact mechanism by which electroshock therapy helps unscramble twisted emotions and thought processes is something no one understands completely even after years of continuing research. Nevertheless, the effectiveness of electroshock treatment is undisputed."[36]

Today, there is an insistence that ECT be given only with informed consent, but in the 1940s to 1950s it was common to coerce people into it with little effort to listen to their fears or resistance to it. In California mental hospitals, it was commonly used for schizophrenics. The line between treatment and punishment was vague, with doctors often deciding to use it for any patient who was noisy, resistant, and generally a problem to institutional order.[37] It is still defended and used as an effective therapy for severe depression, although its usefulness for any other condition, such as schizophrenia, is doubtful.

Electroshock causes persistent memory loss in many people and about 40 percent experience loss of cognitive functions.[38] For some, such as Kitty Dukakis, wife of former Massachusetts governor and 1988 presidential candidate, Michael Dukakis, memory loss was seen an acceptable trade-off for overcoming deep depression.[39] Others have seen it as destroying their lives. One of these latter was Ernest Hemingway, leading American author, who received electroshock at the Menninger Clinic in 1961 and thereafter committed suicide, saying to his biographer, "Well, what is the sense of ruining my head and erasing my memory, which is my capital, and putting me out of business? It was a brilliant cure, but we lost the patient."[40]

Lobotomy: Attacking the Brain with an Ice Pick

The shock therapies did brain damage, although that was not the primary intention. In the 1930s there developed a way of attacking the brain directly, on the theory that by lessening the function of the frontal lobes of the brain, the seat of higher intelligence, the intensity of thought that fueled anxiety could be calmed. Surgery to damage the frontal lobes of the brain was pioneered by Portuguese neurologist Antonio Egas Moniz in 1935. Moniz drilled holes in the patient's skull at the scalp and destroyed tissue in the frontal lobes by injecting alcohol into them. Later, he developed a surgical instrument, which he called the leucotome, that cut brain tissue with a wire loop. In 1949 he received the Nobel Prize in medicine for his work.

American psychiatrist Walter Freeman was the major proponent of lobotomy in the United States. Together with neurosurgeon James W. Watts, Freeman performed the first U.S. lobotomy in 1936 on a 63-year-old woman, Alice Hood Hammatt, who was severely depressed and emotionally agitated. Freeman described her as "a master at bitching and really led her husband a dog's life,"[41] Hammatt became calm and placid after the surgery and was able to direct the work of her household, "although her husband and the maid did most of the work."[42] Freeman proclaimed the operation an outstanding success and soon went on to perform nineteen more, on sixteen women and three men. These too were reported as successes, with anxiety considerably diminished but ability to perform daily tasks unimpaired.

Although initially skeptical, more of the medical establishment was won over to the efficacy of the brain surgery in the 1940s.[43] In the 1950s Freeman became a traveling road show for the operation, visiting more than fifty-five hospitals in twenty-three states and Puerto Rico. He was convinced that this was the only way to relieve the overcrowding of mental hospitals and allow their agitated inmates to return home to live with their families. Freeman perfected a new form of the operation that could be performed in a psychiatrist's office in twenty minutes without anesthetic or a trained surgeon. This was the transorbital lobotomy performed initially with an ice pick from Freeman's own kitchen. The upper eyelid was lifted and a thin instrument was placed against the top of the eye socket and then driven into the brain. It was then moved from side to side to sever the nerve fibers connecting the front lobes to the thalamus. In some cases the instrument was moved upward, sending the tip deeper into the brain to make a deep frontal cut. The instrument was then removed to perform the same motions through the other eye. Eventually Freeman became so efficient with this operation that he could use two hands to do both sides of the brain at once.

Between 1936 and the mid-1960s, about 40,000 lobotomies were performed in the United States, with Freeman personally doing about

10 percent of them. Freeman kept careful notes on each patient and traveled extensively for follow-up visits, seeking to track the effects of the surgery. After more than a decade of checking on the effects of the operations, Freeman estimated that one-third of those who received it were better off, while about 67 percent were unchanged or worsened. About 2 percent died directly from the operations, due to hemorrhages, seizures, or infection.[44]

One has to ask, however, what Freeman counted as improvement? Clearly, he saw some loss of higher intelligence as an acceptable trade-off for "calming" the person and relieving his or her agitated emotional state. Lobotomized persons lost interest in intellectual or creative pursuits and were content with routine activity in the household or simple forms of employment. People "who had once painted pictures, written poetry or composed music were now 'no longer ashamed to fetch and carry, to wait on tables or make beds or empty cans.'"[45]

Among those who should be reckoned as having worsened as a result of the surgery was Rosemary Kennedy, sister of President John F. Kennedy. Rosemary was the oldest of the Kennedy daughters and notably slower than the others, although by no means severely retarded.[46] She was also seen as the most beautiful of the five sisters. In the summer of 1941, when she was twenty-three, she was living in a convent school in Washington, D.C. She had begun to suffer from mood swings and outbursts of anger. Perhaps even more troubling to her father, millionaire Joseph Kennedy, she began to sneak out at night and return in the morning with her clothes bedraggled. The nuns feared she might be picking up men and would become pregnant.

Although Joseph Kennedy allowed considerable latitude in sexual morality for himself and his sons, he had strict ideas of sexual morality for his daughters, most of whom he sent to Catholic convent schools, while his sons went to Harvard.[47] Joe Kennedy began to inquire about the possibility of a lobotomy for Rosemary. His wife, Rose, for whom Rosemary (Rose Marie) was named, asked her daughter Kathleen to look into it. Kathleen was told by a reporter researching St. Elizabeth's Hospital in Washington, D.C., that the results were "just not good," that afterward the patients "don't worry so much, but they are gone as a person, just gone." Kathleen reported back to her mother, saying: "Oh, Mother, no, it's nothing we want done for Rosie."[48] Joe Kennedy nevertheless decided to go through with it. He was turned down by a physician in Boston, but Freeman consented to do it. "As a man who always sought the finest experts," Kennedy was assured by Freeman that it would alleviate Rosemary's problems. Kennedy had it done without Rose's consent, while she was away traveling in California with two of her children, Kathleen and Jack.

The operation was performed in early fall 1941, at George Washington University hospital in Washington, D.C., by Watts and Freeman working as a team. Rosemary was only mildly sedated and was awake during the procedure. "The doctors kept talking to Rosemary, getting her to sing or count. . . . As long as she continued to sing out and to add and subtract, the doctors kept cutting away, destroying a larger and larger area of the brain."[49] The operation left Rosemary reduced to an infantile state, incontinent and unable to speak more than a few words. She was sent to live in Craig House, a private psychiatric hospital north of New York City "famous for its discretion in handling the wealthy and the prominent"[50] and later to St. Coletta's School for Exceptional Children in Wisconsin.

In the years after the operation, Rosemary received few visits from her family. Her mother, Rose, did not see her for twenty years. John Kennedy paid a secret call on her when campaigning in the state in 1958. The one sister who visited her more often was Eunice Kennedy Shriver, who would found the Special Olympics in her name. The Kennedy family thereafter portrayed her as having suffered, from childhood, from severe retardation, rather than having received a lobotomy for mood swings and unruly behavior. Thus, the lobotomy that destroyed Rosemary's mind became a family secret.[51] Before we rage at Joe Kennedy as a domineering sexist (which he undoubtedly was), we have to reflect on the fact that he believed he was acting on the best medical advice. The Rosemary Kennedy case is never mentioned in Walter Freeman's own notations about his patients, although James Watts did consent to give an interview on it in his nineties.[52]

Electroshock therapy has been criticized by feminists as being given to far more women nationally than men and as reinforcing stereotypes of female passivity. Braslow did not find marked gender stereotypes determining who got electroshock therapy in the California hospitals he studied, but he did find that such gender stereotypes played a key role in selecting candidates for lobotomy.[53] Far more women than men were given lobotomies. In the United States as a whole, 60 percent were women, and in California hospitals as many as 85 percent were female, with 89 percent of these receiving repeated and more radical forms of lobotomy.

Lobotomy corresponded to the cultural views of women in the 1940s and 1950s, with women's mental functions seen as more dependent on their bodies than were men's. Any kind of hostile acting out or sexual promiscuity was viewed as more unacceptable in women than men, while being reduced to a passive state capable only of rote household labor more appropriate for female social roles. It was also not uncommon to combine lobotomy with clitoridectomy, in order to curb masturbation and strong sexual urges in women.[54] The Rosemary Kennedy case seems to fit these views of women's proper social and sexual role. One can hardly imagine Joe Kennedy seeking a lobotomy for one of his sons.

Drugs: Fixing the Brain through Chemistry

This presentation of earlier forms of treatment of mental illness may seem to be an exercise in antiquarianism, having no relevance to today, when we have "learned better" and left behind the mistakes of the past. Since the mid-1960s psychotropic drugs have superseded other kinds of treatment of mental illness, with the exception of electroconvulsive therapy, which survives in a more specialized role. Wetpacks, fever therapy, Metrazol and insulin therapy, lobotomy, bleeding and blistering, tranquilizing chairs, and chains (although not all restraints) are now ancient history.

There has been a tendency in the history of psychiatric treatment to defend each of these innovations in turn as the latest in scientific medicine, using them widely and frequently for almost any person defined as "mentally ill," no matter what the diagnosis. Then, when something new comes along that seems to do a better job at the same thing, the former practices are dismissed as belonging to an unenlightened past. Yet the current reliance almost entirely on "meds," or psychotropic drugs, for mental illness reveals much of the same questionable mentality that caused problems in the past. This is the tendency to seek a purely biological or somatic intervention, to construct the "cause" and definition of mental illness in terms of the effects of this particular intervention, and to identify bodily symptoms caused by the intervention as the manifestation of the disease. Any negative feedback by the patients themselves is ignored on the assumption that they lack "insight" into their own illness and are unreliable witnesses to the effects of the somatic interventions on their own bodies and spirits.

In short, there is the tendency to impose a particular physical response as the best available solution, if not complete cure, primarily in terms of how successfully it curtails socially annoying symptoms such as being violent, argumentative, resistant, and sarcastic, and makes the person "calm" and "compliant" with the medical regimen of the day. Psychiatric treatment appears to have little to do with whether or not the person is living a fuller life. As Braslow puts it, "like our predecessors, we are locked into an epistemological framework that cannot easily distinguish between control and cure."[55]

As mentioned in chapter 3, the first neuroleptic drug to be discovered was chlorpromazine, marketed under such names as Thorazine and Largactil. It was used originally to numb those undergoing surgery, and later to calm mental patients. When it was identified as inhibiting the neurotransmitter dopamine, mental illness was then defined as "caused" by an excess of dopamine, which could be "fixed" by repressing excess dopamine activity. In the 1960s a number of antipsychotic drugs appeared on the market, in addition to chlorpromazine. Among the most common are haloperidol (Haldol), thioridazine (Mellaril), trifluoperaine (Stelazine), fluphenazine (Prolixin), perphenazine (Trilafon), thiothixene (Navane), loxapine (Loxitane), and molindone (Moban). All were claimed to work by suppressing excess dopamine activity.

A number of troubling side effects appeared with this first generation of antipsychotic drugs. One of these side effects is acute dystonia or
spasms of tongue, throat, eyes, and neck. A manifestation of this is the
eyes rolling up, something that David has often experienced. Another
side effect is akathisia, or extreme restlessness, resulting in the inability
to sit still and the need to constantly move. David has manifested this
in the constant moving of his legs back and forth and waving his arms
and the need continually to put his arms over his head. Another side
effect is akinesia, or decreased spontaneity. David's passivity may be an
expression of this. Other side effects are pseudo-parkinsonism or symptoms similar to Parkinson's disease: stiffness and tremors, loss of facial
expression and drooling, and tardive dyskinesia, which manifests itself
in involuntary movements of the mouth and tongue, chewing movements, and jerky movements of legs and arms. David was afflicted by
these side effects early on upon receiving medication, but they later
disappeared. Such side effects can be counteracted by taking benztropine (Cogentin), an anticholinergic drug that blocks the neurotransmitter acetylcholine.

In the late 1980s a new generation of antipsychotic drugs began
to appear on the market. Among them are clozapine (Clozaril), ris-
peridone (Risperdal), olanzapine (Zyprexa), quetiapine (Seroquel),
ziprosidone (Geodon), and aripiprazole (Abilfy). I will discuss particularly Clozaril, which David was put on when he was in Hawaii, soon
after it appeared on the market. David has been on Clozaril off and
on since the late 1980s. His prescription on June 4, 2008, was five
100-milligram tablets of clozapine, two ten-milligram tablets of halop-
erdol, and two two-milligram tablets of benztropine to be taken once
a day at night. This represents a reduction of his earlier prescription,
when he was also given an antidepressant and took his pills three times
a day.

As with so many other new medications, Clozaril was hailed as
a "miracle drug" that could clear up the symptoms of those who had
previously been little affected by the other drugs. We did experience
an improved speech coherence on David's part after he began taking
Clozaril. Clozaril is also believed to be much less apt to cause tardive

dyskinesia. But it too had troubling side effects. The most problematic side effect is agranulocytosis, or decreased white blood cells, which can make the body vulnerable to infections. Weekly monitoring of blood counts must be done to guard against this danger. It also causes sedation, excess salivation, and weight gain, all of which are bothersome to David. Increased psychotic symptoms and thoughts of suicide may appear if a person withdraws rapidly from Clozaril.

Research psychiatrist E. Fuller Torrey claims that the antipsychotic drugs are highly effective, with 70 percent of patients clearly improving, 25 percent improving minimally, and 5 percent getting worse.[56] But these figures are less impressive when one realizes that in the 70 percent group seen as improving markedly, there is only a 20 to 50 percent reduction in symptom severity.[57] Our own experience is that many of David's symptoms, such as hearing voices, seem unaffected by the medications.

There is also increasing uncertainty whether the dopamine repression hypothesis actually has anything to do with how these drugs "work." Clozaril, for example, is known to have almost no effect on dopamine. As Torrey puts it:

> The fact is that we do not know precisely how antipsychotic drugs work. Perhaps their major therapeutic effect is on another neurotransmitter system, such as sigma receptors or those utilizing serotonin, histamine, glutamic acid, acetylcholine or noradrenalin. Perhaps their therapeutic effect has little to do with neurotransmitters but is instead dependent on some other property, such as their known antiviral effects.[58]

Torrey shrugs off the importance of knowing just what these drugs are actually doing to the brain. "Since we do not understand yet how aspirin works," he writes, "it should not surprise us that we do not understand how antipsychotics work either."[59] But this question of the actual effects of the drugs on the human brain is regarded less casually by the critics of the drugs, who see them not only as having many dangerous side effects, but actually doing long-term brain damage. It is to this debate that I now turn.

Peter Breggin against the Psychiatric Establishment: Whom Can You Trust?

Peter Breggin is an American psychiatrist who is a trenchant critic of biological psychiatry and neuroleptic medication. Bertram Karon, professor of psychology at Michigan State University, has called Breggin "the conscience of American psychiatry,"[60] but much of the mental health establishment would probably disagree, seeing Breggin as an irresponsible maverick, if they have read his work at all. Breggin is the author of numerous books, among them *Toxic Psychiatry*; *Talking Back to Prozac*; *Talking Back to Ritalin*; *The Heart of Being Helpful*; and *Your Drug May Be Your Problem: How and Why to Stop Taking Psychiatric Medications*. The second edition of his book *Brain-Disabling Treatments in Psychiatry: Drug, Electroshock and the Psychopharmaceutical Complex*,[61] appeared in 2008. Breggin has made himself controversial by his critical writings against neuroleptic and antidepressants drugs, especially their use on children, and by his criticism of the psychopharmaceutical system. He has also been an expert witness in numerous court cases involving tardive dyskinesia caused by psychiatric drugs, brain damage from electroshock, and other issues related to patients' rights.

For Breggin schizophrenia is not a brain disease, and no amount of brain scans has been able to prove that it is. Nor have family studies been able to prove that it is inheritable genetically. Indeed, if it is genetic, it should have long since died out, since schizophrenics have a low reproduction level.[62] Rather, these genetic studies have inadvertently tended to confirm environmental factors as playing the key role. Although he sees abusive family environments as one important factor, a variety of social stresses can be involved, including bullying in school and violence in society and war.

Breggin sees schizophrenia as a failed psychospiritual crisis that particularly afflicts sensitive and poetic people, typically adolescents and young adults who are struggling with the deeper questions of the meaning of life—questions of love, life, and death and God. But instead of being able to emerge from this crisis with some new interpretation of life and vocation to contribute of society's self-understanding, they become over-whelmed by the crisis, stuck in symbolic narratives that sound "crazy" to others, and they retreat into counterproductive coping strategies. What they lack are the right mentors to help guide them to some new stage of coping with this crisis and developing the capacity to take responsibility for their lives, despite whatever damage they may have experienced in the family, in society, or even from the psychiatric establishment.[63]

Breggin is not alone in this view of schizophrenia. Anton Boisen, founder of the field of clinical-pastoral education that put seminary students in training in mental hospitals in the 1920s and 1930s, concluded from his own experience of mental illness, and that of his patients in Worcester and Elgin state mental hospitals, that schizophrenia paralleled the religious experience of crisis in meaning. Studying the great leaders of Christianity, such as the apostle Paul and George Fox, the founder of the Society of Friends, as well as his own experience and that of many patients he knew, Boisen concluded that what is called mental illness today is similar to the deep period of troubling that religious people go through. This period of crisis prepares them for the transforming experience that allows them to reorganize the meaning of life on a new integrated basis and to feel themselves endowed with a sense of mission and purpose.[64] This process of breakdown and transformation is short-circuited by being treated by physiological psychiatric treatments, such as hydrotherapy in mental hospitals, a judgment Boisen would probably have extended to medication.

This description of the onset of adolescent schizophrenia as an overwhelming psychospiritual crisis rings true with our experience with David. Recall, for example, his 1982 reflections on the "causes" of his "problems" (in chapter 3):

> My problem then being that something I feel as deathlike is either present or non-existent, as I can tell that I am happy or sad, dead or alive, good or bad, pretty or ugly, "full" or empty. And I am only sure of something so far: my objection is not to myself. It is to "others." Yet know my problem is real, so I have to look deeper at everything, since I find the world so simple, and say: "Why should I live the way the world is made?" If the world is simple and I am sick, so that life must

be cruel, when I want to make my own world. It is irrelevant whether the world is handed to me on a silver platter, because I don't want it. I want to make my own world and survive that way in order to find out my limitations more truthfully.

David's poem "The Sprig" (p. 98–9) expresses an identification with the struggle of the tiny plant to survive the long, cold Chicago winter, even while protesting its "betrayal" by the "Indian summer" of a warm autumn that fails to warn of the coming freeze. His poem "Making a Friend of a Mannequin" (p. 99–101) expresses a deep sense of the mingling of love and death. The poem written when he was fifteen, "The Desert" (p. 13), speaks of it as a realm of death, *"the Devil's playground, which God has set aside for his alter ego and for those who are strong enough in spirit to rend the veil of civilized illusion and gaze naked into her stark reality."* Presumably, David counted himself at that time as one of those "strong spirits" capable of rending this "veil of civilized illusion."

Rejecting the world as it is and retreating into a world of David's own making seems to reflect graphically what Breggin calls the failed "psychospiritual journey" of someone sensitive to the horrors and betrayals that surrounded him. These included the poverty of inner city Washington, D.C., in blatant contrast to its gleaming official buildings, the drug trips of his friends, and the criticism of the failed Vietnam War. Awareness of these contradictions of American society were ever present in the nation's capital as David grew up there as an adolescent and participated in many antiwar protests.

For Breggin, responding to the manifestations of this psychospiritual crisis with neuroleptic drugs is the worst possible solution. Instead of helping a sensitive youth find his or her way to cope with a traitorous world whose bright facade of promise conceals its deathlike reality, the psychiatric establishment seeks to close down the creative insights that spark such distress. Breggin believes that these psychiatric drugs literally cause a chemical lobotomy. For him, this is not rhetorical exaggeration, but a biological description of how they work.

Just as a surgical lobotomy cuts the nerve fibers between the frontal lobes—the seat of higher human functions of love, concern for others, empathy, self-insight, creativity, initiative, autonomy, rationality, abstract reasoning, judgment, and determination—and the rest of the brain, so neuroleptic drugs interdict the nerve pathways between the frontal lobes and the emotion-regulating limbic system. Thus, they have much the same effect as a lobotomy, creating people who are passive, shallow, and blunted.[65] Such people, while poor public citizens, make fine patients, compliant and nonresistant.

For Breggin, the neuroleptic drugs have many troublesome side effects—shakes, tremors, shuffling gait, and rolling eyes—that the psychiatric establishment has downplayed and minimized as "manageable." More importantly, these side effects are expressions of a terrible secret: that their *main* effect is to do damage to the brain, especially that part of the brain that sustains intelligence and creativity. People who take such drugs for a long time lose a significant part of their higher intelligence, creativity, and initiative, and their brains reflect this diminished capacity due to physical atrophy.[66]

Even though David has been mostly "compliant" with psychiatric drugs prescribed for him by the psychiatric establishment, Breggin's negative view corresponds closely with David's opinion. When he was first given the drug Prolixin, David was initially favorable and believed it would help him, in spite of the opposition of his sister Becky, who opposed and continues to oppose such medication. Thus, he wrote January 10, 1982:

> Have a change in my constitution tonight. If this should continue I will continue: that is, begin taking Prolixin every day, in the afternoon or late morning until I get a head of steam and maybe in the night. In spite of Becky's opinion I begin to feel more strongly that in the long run, in a not very apparent way, Med may help me and has helped, any opinion of Becky nonwithstanding. . . .

Four days later, on January 14, 1982, David's opinion of Prolixin had radically changed. Because Thresholds, the day program he was part of at the time, demanded compliance with medication, he also decided to stop going to this program.

I have decided that I will definitely not take Prolixin. So unless my
parents decide to go along with it as if I were taking Prolixin, I guess
I won't go to Thresholds.

In another reflection on the sources of his sickness written on December 17, 1982, he referred to his problems as having first been precipitated by "the drug scene," but aggravated by medication, the difference between the two being that "marijuana makes one feel better and so does beer, and there is a difference between questioning reality and having no reality (Medication)."

In a plaintive poem written in the 1990s, David reflected on being given psychiatric medication by intravenous injection, creating an illusory hope:

> *Intravenous injection*
> *As the patient goes,*
> *Though all the will and woes.*
> *Tobacco roads,*
> *Instilling sideways shows,*
> *Instilling hope as well as dope,*
> *Knocking on doors that will*
> *Eventually open.*
> *Both sun and moon do protrude,*
> *A little more fortunately,*
> *Likely to move and flow,*
> *Just as the time we passed*
> *Had grand illusions too.*

A long essay David wrote in a mental hospital in 2004 is harsh toward both the drug Haldol and the psychiatric establishment that gives it out, in language that strikingly echoes Breggin (whom David has not read). He had, however, read Ivan Illych's *Disabling Professions*, which he references in this paragraph (see more of this text on pages 63–4):

> *The strongest medicine in the world is Haldol Decononait* [sic: Decano-
> ate]. *That is, because it has no function whatsoever. It is merely a con-*
> *tradictor or far-ranging placebo which sticks all over your nerves and*

makes you hallucinate, being as the brain is cut off electrically. So your circuit is dead for that reason. The retarded motion of brain activity is what doctors crave, for all the manifestations of organic brain waves to be cut at the base and never connected with brain cells such that people use for communication. Memory, drawing conclusions and hallucinating, "brownouts" or whatever you call them are also affected.

    I guess that some people make their living that way, like the doctors. I consider them to be disabling professions, . . .

Recently, David and I were discussing medications. His doctor had of late reduced them in quantity, terminated the antidepressant, and ordered them to be given only once a day at night. But David had decided not to take them anymore.

RR: "What about the meds? What do you think about them?"

David: "I'm not taking them anymore."

RR: "What do they do for you?"

David: "Nothing."

RR: "They don't have any positive effect for you?"

David: "No."

RR: "Well, what negative things do they do to you? What don't you like about them?"

David: "They make you stupid."

On another occasion David seemed to speak more positively (or ambivalently) about medication, saying, "Medication makes you sober."

RR: "What do you mean by sober?"

David: "It makes you very aware. You have to have a strong willpower to cope with medication. Otherwise, it will make you an automaton."

Since that conversation David has gone back and forth on the question of taking medication. He began to take it again, and then when he felt it made him sick, he declared again that he would not take it. I urged him to discuss his views and experiences of medication with his psychiatrist during his fifteen-minute meeting once every two months. But he declared that discussing this issue with a psychiatrist is useless since "he is paid to give out medication." In other words, for David, his relation to his psychiatrist has nothing to do with establishing any communication. A psychiatrist is only a pill-pusher, and no conversation about this is possible.

On one of David's brief visits with his psychiatrist to prescribe his medication, I sent him in with a note telling the psychiatrist that the medication often made David feel sick and "hung over," and that perhaps he needed less of it. I suggested that maybe David was "aging out," and was beginning to have fewer symptoms. David and the psychiatrist had about a ten-minute conversation on the subject and then the psychiatrist called me in to consult with the two of them. The psychiatrist dismissed the idea that schizophrenics "age out." In a somewhat textbook manner, he explained that there are three kinds of schizophrenia: a single episode and then no more symptoms; a series of episodes with periods of no symptoms in between; and chronic symptoms. He then said, "Since we see the patient only occasionally, we cannot adjust for periods with no symptoms, so we just keep the same dosage."

I was astonished. The royal "we" seemed to be a way of speaking for the established practice of all psychiatrists. In other words, what he was saying is that psychiatrists have such limited and occasional contact with schizophrenic patients that they just prescribe medication for them as if they all had chronic, lifelong symptoms, ignoring the periods when they might have no symptoms. After saying this the psychiatrist agreed to phase out the Haldol and Cogentin as unnecessary and prescribe only Clozaril. After we exited from the psychiatrist's office, I asked David if he felt he had had a positive conversation with him. David shrugged his shoulders and repeated his view that psychiatrists are only there to push pills. "That is what they are paid to do," he said.

On another occasion David told me that the psychiatrist had asked him if he had attended high school, a question that David saw as demeaning and refused to answer. Although I continue to encourage

David to actually talk to his psychiatrist, such a question indicates how little this psychiatrist actually knows about the adult man for whom he has been prescribing medication for more than two years.

As a parent who is trying to be an informed advocate for a son diagnosed with schizophrenia, I find the contradictions about psychiatric drugs create an acute personal dilemma. On the one hand there are the solid ranks of the mental health establishment: medical researchers, authoritative writers, doctors, and the staffs of hospitals, nursing homes, and board-and-care homes determined that these drugs are absolutely essential for someone like David to "function." Although admittedly not a "cure," they are the best thing we have, and any minute now much better drugs will be found.

On the other hand there is Breggin's view, who also knows the research and has worked with patients for more than fifty years, and a number of others who agree with him[67] that these drugs not only do more harm than good, they actually are disabling. They are damaging to the brain and cause a person to lose intelligence, creativity, and initiative. The response of the psychiatric establishment is to dismiss Breggin and his ilk as simply wrong and disreputable. David's own experience and opinion is ambivalent, although mostly in line with these critics, but his views would be dismissed by the psychiatric establishment as evidence that he "has no insight into his illness."

While acting on the "best medical advice," have we all been collaborating in a crime against the humanity of those treated with such drugs? Although I too have mostly been convinced to accept the view that David must take some, although perhaps less, of these medications, I have never been entirely comfortable with the way they have been promoted in the medical system as I have encountered it. From the beginning I was puzzled by the language of needing to make David "medication compliant." If you experience a drug as helpful, you don't have to be made "compliant." Your own experience makes you willing to take the drug. As a lifelong asthmatic I don't have to be exhorted to take "my meds." I know if I don't, I will wheeze and be out of breath when I do daily tasks.

Clearly, these meds do not make David, and many other patients in the mental health system, feel good. In fact they make him twitch, roll his eyes, and feel lethargic, and after thirty years of taking them, he is sure that they "make you stupid." It is a wonder he has mostly taken them and has not revolted sooner and more insistently. Except for a few days in January 1982, David has taken his medications, not because he thought they could help him but because he saw himself as caught in a system that insisted that he take them, that would even inject him intravenously with them if he did not take them by mouth.

After thirty years of taking antipsychotic drugs, David has lost a considerable part of the intelligence he had at eighteen. He has no capacity to sit in a classroom and now seldom reads, which was once his great pleasure. He is highly passive and has little initiative beyond basic needs of washing himself and (usually) getting to meals. His major activity has been concentrated on finding ways to come home, either walking, catching the bus, or riding his bike. He still has a certain sparkle, a sense of humor and irony at the situations around him. He can engage in insightful comments about the dreary board-and-care home where he was living and about his fellow patients and staff. He is remarkable in his memory for Spanish, for words and names of authors from past reading, and for being able to spell difficult words. He can still be fun to be with, but he is a much-diminished human being.

Again I ask, is this really the effect of his "disease" or the effect of thirty years of medication and a repressive social environment? Recent research on schizophrenia sees the disease itself as causing "brain deterioration." According to Jeffrey Libermann of Columbia University:

> [E]xcessive release of neurotransmitters such as dopamine and glutamate induces a toxic reaction that erodes the gray matter, the cells of the cerebral cortex, the higher thinking center of the brain. Drugs currently available can quell symptoms of psychosis, but cannot repair brain damage once the process has begun. The cognitive defects incurred cannot, at present, be reversed.[68]

Libermann does not discuss whether medication itself, plus a stultifying environment, contributes to this brain deterioration.

The Corruption of the Psychiatric System: Money, Power, and Prestige

The urgency of this question of the brain-damaging effects of medication is aggravated by continual evidence of how corrupted the psychiatric establishment is by money, prestige, and the need to secure the reputation of being impeccably "scientific."

The psychiatric-pharmaceutical complex refers to a powerful system in which large multinational pharmaceutical companies that control and market the major neuroleptic drugs play a major role in funding the professional organizations, journals, research, and medical education of psychiatrists. Who are these pharmaceutical companies? I will name a few of the major ones. There is GlaxoSmithKline, who bought the rights to chlorpromazine (Thorazine) from its French developers and did the image makeover to market it in the United States and around the world as the first antipsychotic wonder drug. GlaxoSmithKline has roots in earlier companies going back to 1880. It is the world's second largest pharmaceutical company, with worldwide sales in 2007 of £7.6 billion ($12.6 billion) and 110,000 employees.

Bristol-Myers Squibb is also a huge multinational pharmaceutical company, with roots in companies going back to 1887 and is a Fortune 500 company. It developed and markets the major neuroleptics Haldol and Prolixin. It also markets the second-generation neuroleptic Abilify, with the Japanese company Otsuka, which invented this drug. Another important company is Janssen, a subsidiary of the huge New Jersey–based health products company Johnson & Johnson. Janssen specializes in mental health drugs and markets the second-generation neuroleptic drug Risperidome. It controls some seventy-five medications connected with mental health and works in 150 countries worldwide.

Another important company is Sandoz, a subsidiary of Novartis. It is a multinational company based in Germany. In 2007 its sales in the United States alone were $7.2 billion. It has 23,000 employees and works in 130 countries. Its major neuroleptic drugs are Clozaril and Mellaril. There is also Pfizer, a company focusing on research and development.

It is based in New York City and is No. 1 in pharmaceutical sales world-wide. It markets such important neuroleptics as Navane and Geodon. It also controls popular drugs such as Viagra (for male sexual problems) and the widely used cholesterol-lowering drug Lipitor. Finally, I mention (this is not an exhaustive list) Eli Lilly, the tenth largest pharmaceutical company in the world, with revenues of $18 billion in 2007. It was founded by chemist Eli Lilly in 1876 in Indianapolis, Indiana, and is still headquartered there. It markets the second-generation neuroleptic olanzapine (Zyprexa).[69]

The big drug companies largely underwrite the psychiatric establishment. This is true of organized medicine generally in the United States.[70] But it is particularly insidious in psychiatry, since it leads to an exclusive favoring of biological approaches to psychological problems, particularly medication. This is what American Psychiatric Association President Steven Sharfstein called the "bio-bio-bio model" rather than a bio-psycho-social model.[71] The American Psychiatric Association, the major representative of American psychiatry, depends on big drug companies to pay for its newspapers and journals through advertisements and to underwrite its national conferences through booths, seminars, and entertainment.[72]

The Federal Food and Drug Administration (FDA), responsible for approving the safety of all drugs in the United States, is also heavily beholden to big drug companies. Most of the advisors of the FDA, particularly those connected with psychiatry, have ties to the psychopharmaceutical industry.[73] According to Breggin, "All of the studies involved in the FDA approval process are designed completely by the drug companies and conducted by physicians hired and paid for by them." The FDA also is biased toward the drug companies in follow-up studies and complaints after a drug is marketed. In Breggin's view, "When it comes to warning about the dangers of psychiatric drugs, the FDA is more responsive to the profit needs of industry than the safety needs of patients."[74]

The National Institute of Mental Health (NIMH), the federal agency funded to promote mental health in the United States, is also heavily obligated to the drug companies and has become a research institute primarily "on behalf of biological psychiatry and the drug companies."[75]

NIMH publishes a great deal of literature on mental illness, such as its pamphlet "Schizophrenia,"[76] which promotes the view of schizophrenia as a "brain disease" to be cured primarily by medication.

Departments of psychiatry of medical schools also depend heavily on the drug companies for research grants, funding for professorships, and support for projects. They have been taken over by the biomedical approach. Professors at the schools sit on the boards of drug companies and act as consultants for research and development companies funded by the pharmaceutical companies that test the drugs and design the marketing campaigns for them. For-profit clinical testing companies have sprung up that are totally funded by the companies who conduct the supposedly "scientific" studies designed to prove the superiority of a new drug about to be marketed by the company over an earlier one.[77] Many journal articles in the major psychiatric journals that teachers and working psychiatrists rely on for "objective" information actually arise from such studies funded by the drug companies.[78] Doctors, including psychiatrists, need to do regular continuing education to maintain their licenses, and much of this accredited continuing education is done by drug companies.[79]

The medical insurers are also affected by drug company money, since they reimburse primarily for drugs, electroshock, and psychiatric hospitalization, but pay little or nothing for psychotherapy and social rehabilitation, crisis centers, or housing.[80] This bias toward a purely biomedical approach to mental health has had a significant effect on the *Diagnostic and Statistical Manual of Mental Disorders*, the official manual published by the American Psychiatric Association, on which psychiatrists rely for diagnosis of mental illnesses. As Herb Kutchins and Stuart Kirk have shown in their book *Making Us Crazy: DSM: The Psychiatric Bible and the Creation of Mental Disorders*,[81] the *DSM* has grown from a slim pamphlet in 1952 (the first edition) to a 943-page tome in the revised fourth edition of 2000.

This growth reflects the endless expansion of areas of daily life categorized as "mental disorders." These now include "eating disorders," "sleeping disorders," "adjustment disorders," and "personality disorders." Even shyness has been construed as a mental disorder.[82]

The way these disorders are described is geared toward qualifying for insurance reimbursements for these diagnoses and treatments, which invariably emphasize medication. Many of the advisors of the *DSM* are connected to the drug companies, and each expansion of an area of daily life labeled as a mental illness becomes a new category of medication to be developed and marketed by the pharmaceutical companies. One of the major growth areas is medications for young children supposedly afflicted by attention-deficit disorders, depression, and other kinds of anxieties.[83]

This problem shows no signs of being corrected. In 2008 the American Psychiatric Association embarked on a new (fifth) revision of the *DSM* to appear in 2012. This process is being severely criticized by some psychiatrists because of its secrecy, with members of committees sworn to confidentiality. These critics fear that the tendency to make new categories of mental illness with an eye to insurance policies and funding for new psychiatric drugs will continue in the new revision.[84]

This substantial corruption of the psychiatric establishment by drug companies, and the bias toward the biomedical model and medication as the solution, creates a severe problem of trust for the family advocate of a diagnosed mental patient. One can expect that psychiatrists prescribing medication will ignore the side effects—and perhaps even main effect—of neuroleptic drugs as possibly damaging to the brain, as well as ignoring the general health of one's family member. One can assume that concern for psychosocial needs, employment, housing, and soul nurture of this person will be disregarded and that resources and information on such matters will be unavailable in community clinics.

Additionally, one can assume that alternatives, such as dietary approaches, will be scoffed at by psychiatrists, or they will simply declare themselves unacquainted with information on the subject. Even NAMI (National Alliance on Mental Illness), the primary organization set up to represent family and friend advocates, has taken drug money for their campaigns against discrimination and promotes medication as the major solution.[85] Thus, family advocates, including me, feel very much alone in seeking advice and help that they can trust.

Living Arrangements

Recovery or Maintenance?

Over the course of David's thirty-five-year struggle with mental illness, Herman and I have been frustrated time and again in our efforts to secure suitable living arrangements for our son. By "living arrangements" I do not mean simply physical housing, but an environment that embodies the nurture and relationships every human being needs. Like the many people with mental illness, David's experience encompasses a variety of institutions, including mental hospitals, board-and-care facilities, nursing homes, medical health clinics, and, briefly, homeless shelters and even jail. All have been defined by frighteningly limited resources and—even more—by limited vision. I am not interested in vilifying these institutions or the individuals running them. I think, by and large, they are doing the best they can. As a historian, I am interested in presenting how the options for people with mental illness have improved little over nearly three centuries. As a parent, I am dedicated to finding something better for David and for all who suffer from this terrible disease.

Family and Community Care

In colonial times the responsibility for caring for people with mental illness belonged to families. Authorities stepped in only when family was absent or when it was clear that they could not provide the necessary care. Through the centuries a large percentage of people with mental illness have remained with their families or have been returned to their families after being released from other institutions, such as mental hospitals. Staying with family, however, does not necessarily ensure good care. People with mental illness were sometimes hidden away—even locked in attics or basements—by their families. If the existence of such a person became known, a town council might authorize the head of family to build a small prison next to the family home in which to incarcerate him or her. So it was in 1689 that the town council of Braintree, Massachusetts, authorized one Samuel Speere to "build a little house 7 foot long and 5 foot wide & set it by his house to secure his Sister good wife Witty being distracted & provide for her."[1]

Living with family remains a major means for housing people with mental illness today. NAMI (National Alliance on Mental Illness) reported after conducting a survey of their members that 42 percent of seriously ill people were living with a family member. This is probably an overestimate of the total number, since the survey comprised NAMI members who are committed to being family advocates. E. Fuller Torrey estimates that 500,000 or about 28 percent of people with mental illness live with their families.[2] In the early twenty-first century, however, living with family means something different than it did in earlier times. In the United States today, people with mental illness who live at home have access to Supplemental Security Income (SSI) and Medicaid, which can be used to partly reimburse family for room and board. These funds can also be used to cover medical expenses, including psychiatric medications. If willing and able, family members can be named legal guardians for family members with mental illness. In this role they administer federal and state benefits and see to it that those with mental illness take their "meds."

Boarding Out

In colonial times town councils might "board out" a person with mental illness who had no family or whose family could not provide the care needed. Boarding out involved contracting with another family who, for a small stipend, would take the person in and provide the care needed. This led to a remarkable practice, influenced by the institution of slavery, which continued into the middle of the nineteenth century. Paupers, including those with mental illness, were put up for public auction by the town or county. Townspeople could then bid for them, with the auctioned people awarded to the lowest bidder, ensuring that the municipality would only pay the least for care. Those who took such people in for a fee could then use them in any way they wanted, primarily as unpaid labor. Farmers particularly were on the lookout for able-bodied poor people, including the more docile among "the retarded" or "mentally ill," who could be used for farm labor.[3]

Boarding out continues today, though people with mental illness are no longer auctioned off. Rather, families or small groups of entrepreneurs make arrangements to take in people with mental illness. The providers receive SSI housing reimbursements for providing room and board and managing the boarders' medications and hospitalizations. By housing people two to four in a room, and having a low-paid staff and inexpensive food, such board-and-care homes become for-profit businesses. At present, board-and-care facilities house perhaps a fifth of those with mental illness.[4]

In our experience it is immigrants—often Filipinos with some nursing or medical training—who take on the difficult work of caring for people with mental illness in American society. In the United States, board-and-care homes come in different sizes. Some facilities are large, professional institutions for a hundred persons. Others are run by families, who add a couple of rooms to their own homes and take in four or six mental patients. These small board-and-care homes seem to be the preferred option for the mental health system in Hawaii.

The larger board-and-care facilities often have some gestures in the direction of recreation and education, with a room set aside for teaching basic math and English, coloring pictures or playing games, such as bingo. Some organize the residents to make their beds and clean their rooms, and see that they go out to day programs. Others, by expecting nothing other than minimal compliance with house rules, inculcate idleness and dependency. None, in my experience, creates anything that one might call work, either in caring for the facility itself or involving the persons in some job-training program. This differs from colonial times, when people with mental illness were made to work to pay for their care. Today they are valued for the government subsidies they bring with them.

Prior to moving to his current residence in March 2009, David lived in four board-and-care facilities after returning to California six years earlier. In the last home David seemed to have friendly relations with many other residents whom he greeted by name. He moved in with an older Hispanic man who seemed especially pleased to have the large easy chair, television, microwave, refrigerator, coffee maker, wall posters, and floor carpet that David brought with him. The man spoke no English, but David can still manage some Spanish, so they got on well. However, as time passed it became harder for David to spend a full day at his residence. He lived for our visits and thanked us often for being willing to take him on excursions or to let him spend time in our home.

Dumping

Dumping the poor, particularly those afflicted with mental illness or mental retardation, was a common practice among local authorities in the past that has returned today. In colonial times town authorities would rid their communities of unwanted people by challenging their residency. Wandering people with no family to claim them or any way of proving their residency were driven to a community at some distance where they were dumped off and left to fend for themselves. The assumption was that their incoherence would prevent them from informing the authorities in another community of their identity or where they came from.

Today, an area in downtown Los Angeles that includes a number of services for those who are homeless or drug- or alcohol-addicted has become a dumping ground for people who are released from jails, hospitals, and health care centers but who have no plans for where to go next. Police officers from communities around Los Angeles and the more distant areas served by the LAPD, including Hollywood and West Los Angeles, drop people off on Skid Row. Hospitals and health care centers also engage in this practice when people are released and have no place to go. These vulnerable people are delivered to Skid Row in police cars, ambulances, and taxis.[5]

David has never been dumped, but he was abandoned once by the authorities responsible for arranging secure transportation for him to a new residence. After being released from a psychiatric ward, David waited as he was told to be picked up and delivered to his new residence. After considerable waiting, David set off on his own, not knowing, of course, where he was supposed to go. He wandered the city for five days without money, food, or water. The hospital made no effort to confirm that he arrived at his new residence or to notify us that David had been released. David wasn't dumped by the authorities, but he was lost by hospital personnel.

Poorhouses

The poorhouse was another past institution for the indigent, including people with mental illness. Historian David Wagner has noted that the poorhouse is a largely forgotten institution in American social history.[6] If it is mentioned to most Americans, they might think of it as something that existed in the colonial period or, at the latest, into the mid-nineteenth century. They would be surprised to learn that it has a more than 300-year history in the United States. The first one was built in 1660 as Boston's workhouse and the last ones were converted into other institutions in the 1970s. The heyday of the poorhouse was in the 1820s to 1930s. At their height there were as many as 2,300 poorhouses in the United States. They were county or city institutions under local control. In the 1820s there was an effort to see that every county had one.[7]

The poorhouse was a mixture of charity and punishment that brought together many indigent populations: orphaned children, pregnant girls thrown out by their families, women fleeing from domestic violence, poor widows and the elderly, people with physical handicaps and those with mental illness, drunks and petty thieves, able-bodied people down on their luck, and people too poor to heat their homes in winter who used the poorhouse for seasonal housing. It became the source of many other institutions in American life: jails, nursing homes, orphanages, domestic-violence shelters, homes for unwed mothers, mental hospitals, and, today, the homeless shelter, as different groups were separated out into specialized institutions.

The impetus for the poorhouse in America came from England, where it was part of the "poor laws" intended to discipline the rural peasantry evicted from their land by enclosure movements and to force them into employment in the industrializing economy. In England this took the form of the workhouse or the house of correction, to which paupers and vagrants were sentenced for a fixed term and forced to work. In the American colonies and the early United States, this situation did not exist in the same way as in England, and so only a few of the poorhouses were really organized as workhouses.

One of these was Boston's House of Industry, erected in 1823, as a place of forced employment for the "able-bodied poor." It rapidly deteriorated into a custodial institution. Thus, in 1833, ten years after its founding, it was described in discouraged tones in a report to the Massachusetts legislature:

> Instead of being a House of Industry, the institution has become at once, a general Infirmary—an Asylum for the insane and a refuge for the deserted and most destitute children of the city. So great is the proportion of the aged and infirm, of the sick insane, idiots and helpless children in it, that nearly all the effective labor of the females and much of that of the males, is required for the care of those who cannot take care of themselves.[8]

Poorhouses came in many sizes, from a large farm house in which thirty to fifty people were squeezed to a group of buildings housing as many as 300. One county poorhouse described in a report to the New York legislature in 1838 held 174 inmates, among them ten "lunatics" and eight "idiots." One unheated garret room held twenty-five men and boys, among them two "insane" people, sharing eleven beds. Another unheated garret held twelve women and children, including one "lunatic" crowded into five beds. A tiny room of seventeen feet by nine feet held ten women and children sharing three beds. Another chamber held two "lunatics" chained to the floor at opposite sides of the room.[9]

At its best a poorhouse could be a homelike refuge for the destitute. A farmer and his wife might accept the county fees to make their farmhouse into a poorhouse, in which thirty or forty inmates might reside, eating together with the farmer's wife and children. The women and girls were likely put to work processing products of the garden, preparing meals, and cleaning the house, while the men labored with the farmer in the fields. As a big family they might sing together around the piano, groups might play cards together in the evening, and the children of the destitute would grow up with the farmer's children as siblings.[10] The fact that there was little separation between the farmer's family, the few paid staff, and the different kinds of "inmates" contributed to this homelike possibility. Although often overcrowded and punitive, for many it was the best option available.

But for most Americans, being "driven to the poorhouse" was a horrible fate. It was from the terrible scandal of the poorhouse that reformers sought to rescue people with mental illness in the mid-nineteenth century, setting up asylums and hospitals specializing in the care of the "insane." These institutions defined themselves as not just custodial but as curative; that is, as medical institutions that would address insanity as a "disease." Yet, many poorhouses lingered into the late 1930s until the advent of the Social Security laws of the New Deal. The last ones closed in the 1960s and early 1970s with the development of SSI for the disabled. Many of the same buildings that had been poorhouses were converted into either jails or nursing homes, thus collapsing into the opposite ends of their original origins.

However oppressive and stigmatized as they may have been, Wagner sees the poorhouses of the past as comparing favorably with the homeless shelters that serve the poorest in American cities today. The poorhouse was funded by the county, while homeless shelters are often run as volunteer charities by churches. The poorhouse, however crowded, gave their inmates a full-time place to stay, while most homeless shelters provide an evening meal and a pallet on the floor in a crowded room for only a night. People can enter them only at the end of the day and must leave in the morning, perhaps with something for breakfast in their hand. No matter how cold the weather, such poor in the United States today are homeless during the daylight hours, perhaps seeking other drop-in centers or charitable kitchens for lunch and shelter during the day.[11] Usually, they do not even have a locker of their own where they might keep a few belongings during the daylight hours; instead, they must carry everything they own on their backs or in pushcarts.

After a succession of expulsions from board-and-care homes in Hawaii, David stayed briefly in a homeless shelter in downtown Honolulu. Fortunately, in the Hawaii mental health system, each client is assigned a social worker who follows the client from one address to the next. David's social worker rescued him from the shelter, sent him to a hospital, and then helped him get back to us in Illinois.

The Invention of Asylum and the Mental Hospital

The end of the eighteenth and early nineteenth centuries saw the birth of a reform movement for the treatment of people with mental illness. Philippe Pinel in France and Vincenzo Chiarugi in Italy advocated striking off the chains of "the insane" and treating them in a humane manner.[12] More influential in the United States was the development of the York Retreat founded by Quakers in England in 1792. Several mental hospitals had already been founded in England in the preceding decades, among them the York Asylum in 1777. In 1791 a member of the York Friends Meeting, Hannah Mills, died there under circumstances that suggested ill treatment. Friends were not allowed to visit her in her last days. This incident prompted William Tuke, member of the York Friend's Meeting, to propose that the Friends set up their own asylum where fellow Friends could find loving and humane treatment.

Tuke convinced other Friends both from York and nationwide to contribute, and the York Retreat opened its doors in 1796 with thirty patients. Key to Tuke's idea of moral treatment was a healing environment. The rooms would be sunny, clean, and orderly, looking out on twenty-seven acres of gardens where the recovering might stroll. There would be stimulating activities: music; a drama society; sports, such as tennis and croquet; gentle work activities, such as hand work for women and gardening and a print shop for men. The model of therapy was initially nonmedical, for Tuke saw little of value in the current medical treatment of the mentally ill that featured purging, blistering, and bleeding.

The leadership of the Retreat was in the hands of laypeople, rather than doctors. Restraints were avoided except as a last resort, when a patient might be confined to his or her room for a while or even put in a straitjacket. The Quakers approached their patients with a conviction that there was a divine spark in every person that may have been obscured but was not destroyed by their illness. Through creating a "brotherhood of love," the insane could be healed.[13]

Although the York Retreat would grow in size over the next 200 years, expanding to more than a hundred patients and taking on increasing numbers of non-Quaker patients, and accepting medical leadership and treatments, it would retain its atmosphere of cleanliness, order, pleasant surroundings, and loving care. The York Retreat became a model for reformers around the world of how asylums should be run. Visitors came from across Britain, Europe, and the United States as if on a pilgrimage.[14] The York Retreat still exists today. Its Web site proclaims: "The present day Retreat seeks to retain the original principles behind the early moral treatment practiced here, whilst being responsive to what is best in latest clinical expertise and practice."[15]

New asylums that were founded and old ones that were reformed sought to emulate the style and philosophy of the Retreat. The American Friends were important in carrying the vision of the York Retreat to the United States. The Friend's Asylum, founded by the Philadelphia Society of Friends in Frankford, Pennsylvania, in 1817, sought to follow its guidelines.

The next fifty years would see a continual process of building mental hospitals in the United States. Initially, many of these were private, catering to the middle-class paying patient. But the trend was toward each of the states founding a mental hospital. Funding for institutions for

those with mental illness was shifting from counties and private endow-
ment to state legislatures. A key figure in the promotion of state mental
hospitals was Dorothea Dix (1802–1887), who in the last forty years of
her life crusaded tirelessly on behalf of those with mental illness. She
sought to rescue them from brutal treatment in jails and poorhouses
and to persuade states to found hospitals where those with mental illness could be cared for properly. In her campaign she echoed the words
of her friend and fellow educator Horace Mann, who declared that "the
insane are the wards of the State."

Taking her plea to the nation's Capitol in 1848, Dix sought to persuade Congress to allot government land to each state on which to build
state hospitals. Her plea concluded with these words:

> I ask for the thirty states of the Union, 5,000,000 acres of land, of
> the many hundreds of millions of public lands, appropriated in such
> a manner as shall assure the greatest benefits to all who are in cir-
> cumstances of extreme necessity, and who, through the providence of
> God, *are wards of the nation*, claimants on the sympathy and care of
> the public, through the miseries and disqualifications brought upon
> them by the sorest afflictions with which humanity can be visited.[16]

Twenty states responded to her appeals by establishing or expanding
a state mental hospital—and in some cases more than one. Thirty-two
hospitals were begun or expanded through her influence. This included
a role in the founding of St. Elizabeth's Hospital, the Government Hospital for the Insane, in Washington, D.C. Dix herself sought asylum in
her last years in her "first-born child," the New Jersey State Hospital at
Trenton, where she died on July 17, 1887.[17]

The Big Mental Hospital Routinized

By 1880 the mental hospital had become the accepted place of care for
all "insane" who could not be kept at home. In that year a census showed
that there were 91,997 insane persons out of an American population of
50 million. Of those, 9,300 lived in poorhouses. The remaining 82,697
were divided evenly between living at home and in mental hospitals.

In 1883 there were eighty-three local and state hospitals and one federal institution (St. Elizabeth's). These hospitals varied in size. The nine largest had an average of 1,254 patients, while the nine smallest had an average of 140 patients each. But the trends were clearly toward the large institution of more than 1,000.[18]

The typical nineteenth-century American state mental hospital was constructed according to the "Kirkbridge Plan," the architectural embodiment of the curative therapy current in U.S. psychiatry.[19] This architectural design featured a palatial-looking central building of several stories that held the kitchen, storerooms, reception areas, business and medical offices, chapel, library, and living quarters for the medical officers. Extending laterally on both sides of this central edifice were wings for the patients, also of several stories, one for men and one for women. If more room was needed, additional wings could be built either at right angles or behind these lateral wings.

The patient wings in turn were divided into a number of separate departments and subdepartments, or wards, reflecting the classification of patients primarily by behavior. There were separate departments for quieter patients, for the "demented," and for "melancolics." There were others for the noisy and disturbed, for the suicidal, and for those who were filthy in their habits—those who smeared feces on themselves or on the walls and furniture. These departments allowed the administration both to assign patients into a hierarchy of different behavioral classifications and also to move them up or down as their behavior "improved" or "deteriorated."

This hierarchy of wards also reflected a hierarchy of privileges and disprivileges. Privileges included being able to walk around the grounds or even have released time in the local town, being able to participate in a drama club or sports, or have a work assignment. Disprivileges meant losing these outlets, being limited to a locked ward, confined by restraints, and denied opportunities for work and recreation. No matter how "crazy," those admitted to these institutions quickly grasped the significance of the sections of the building where they were assigned, and they learned how to move up in the system by cooperating with its behavioral expectations. Only those moving to the highest level of behavioral classification could expect to be released as "cured," while those who fell to the lower levels might be confined indefinitely, even lifelong.[20] Thus, while intended to motivate patients to "improve" their behavior and so presumably their mental health, these classification patterns actually tended to reinforce ways of behaving that were functional within the hospital as a "total institution," although dysfunctional elsewhere.

The Failure of the Mental Hospital

In the second half of the nineteenth century, the large American mental hospital was still thought of as the heir of "moral" treatment. Typically, it was located in the countryside with some pleasant-looking grounds around it. There were stimulating activities, such as education or participation in a sports team or a drama reading. Work for women consisted in helping in the laundry and sewing clothes and bedding, while men did outdoor work. Many hospitals had farms attached to them, and reisdents were expected to defray costs by growing some of their own food. But these activities were seen primarily as therapeutic rather than economic. They also became part of the system of privileges to be denied or granted, depending on how patients did or did not conform to behavioral norms. Work was unpaid, but nevertheless sought after by many patients who wanted to "better" themselves.

What continually belied even this "moral vision" was the failure of state legislatures to grant sufficient funds for upkeep of the building and for trained staff. Buildings deteriorated. Broken windows and leaking roofs were not repaired. The numbers of those admitted constantly exceeded the number of beds, so some slept on the floor or on chairs in the day rooms. Attendants worked long hours for low pay, so there was constant turnover. People with little training were recruited and the ratio of patients to staff grew, so that in practice the attendants spent much of their time subduing unruly patients and keeping some from hitting other patients and staff. Not infrequently this meant reciprocal violence by the staff against resistant patients, which resulted in injuries and even death. In short, under the surface of a theory of planned hierarchical order, chaos often ruled.[21]

The nonmedical vision of loving care by laypeople with high human sensibilities of the early York Retreat was long since disregarded in American and English asylums. It was understood that these were medical institutions, and the doctors, with their understanding of insanity as a "brain disease," were firmly in control. Although lacking the psychotropic drugs of our current times, doctors in the late nineteenth century had a variety of sedatives and hypnotics available to them: opium, morphine, chloral hydrate. These were used freely to keep patients "calm" and were seen as "chemical restraints" parallel to the use of physical restraints.

In the 1930s more robust medical interventions became available for treating and controlling people with mental illness. These included fever therapy, insulin, Metrazol and electroshock, and lobotomy, and all were used widely in American hospitals. Henry Cotton, medical director for the New Jersey State Hospital, became convinced that insanity was caused by infection lodged in teeth, tonsils, and intestines. Out of an obsession to prove this theory, Cotton performed countless operations to remove teeth, tonsils, and other organs of the patients in his care, sometimes causing injury and even death. He was so sure of his theory that he even removed his own teeth and those of his children to ward off the possibility of becoming insane. Cotton was an autocrat who possessed near absolute power in running the New Jersey state mental hospital. In this regard he was little different from the directors of other such institutions at that time. Complaints about Cotton and calls to investigate his abuses piled up, but his colleagues in the psychiatric profession were unwilling to entertain any serious critique of what he was doing.[22]

The Critique and Emptying of Mental Hospitals: New Options

The number of patients in mental hospitals in the United States peaked in 1955 at 560,000 inmates, many of whom were elderly and had been in these hospitals for many years. In the decade following World War II, there was a steady stream of criticism of the mental hospital as an institution. Most of critics did not envision shutting them down; they simply wanted more funds to be allotted to improve them, to repair the buildings, and to allow a better staff-patient ratio and better trained, more caring staff. There were some critics, including Erving Goffman, who suggested that mental hospitals created mental illness rather than cured it.[23] Others, in the more radical antipsychiatry movement, claimed there was no such thing as mental illness, that this was only a label created to control and marginalize the deviant.[24]

By 1945 the diversion of funds and medical personnel and staff for the war effort had put mental hospitals in particularly bad shape. A sizable group of conscientious objectors from religious traditions, such as Mennonites and Quakers, had been allowed to do alternative service in mental hospitals during the war, and they were horrified by what they saw. They made strenuous efforts to tell others about these abuses, and soon several journalists were engaged in writing books and articles on the subject.

One particularly important of these exposés of the mental hospital was written by Albert Deutsch, author of a major history of the treatment of mental illness in America.[25] Deutsch investigated six major mental hospitals: Byberry or the Philadelphia State Hospital, the Cleveland State Hospital, the Manhatten State Hospital of New York City, Napa State Hospital in California, Rockland State Hospital in New York, and Georgia State Hospital in Milledgeville, Georgia. With photos and graphic descriptions, he described the aged rotting buildings with broken windows, leaky ceilings, and stained floors. He showed the chronic overcrowding, with people sleeping on floormats in dayrooms and porches. Many were naked or with scanty clothing. Most spent their days in vacuous idleness without work, while some did slave labor in laundries. The food was cold and tasteless, emerging from small, grimy kitchens. There were inadequate, poorly paid staffs, some of whom were recruited from criminal backgrounds and freely beat patients or failed to intervene when some patients hit others. Patients were tied for long hours in restraints on beds or in chairs. There was a basic lack of sanitation, with feces and urine on floors and walls that remained uncleaned. The chronically mentally ill, the senile elderly, and children were mixed together. This horrifying picture, with its photo illustrations, was published in 1948 as *The Shame of the States* and created an instant sensation.[26]

From State to Federal Responsibility

The end of World War II saw the first of a series of pieces of federal legislation that began to shift responsibility and funding for mental health from the states to the federal government. In 1946, under the Truman administration, Congress passed the National Mental Health Act, which put responsibility for research on mental health within the National Institutes of Health. The act envisioned research grants for the diagnosis and treatment of mental disorders and for training of mental health personnel, as well as grants to the states to set up local clinics and to fund demonstration studies on diagnosis and treatment. The act also set up the National Institute of Mental Health (NIMH) as a government agency. During this period, funding for NIMH would expand continually, from $9 million in 1949 to $184 million in 1964.[27]

The next major initiative on mental health took place during the Kennedy administration. The Kennedy siblings had a keen interest in the issue of mental health because of the tragedy of their sister Rosemary, although the focus of Eunice Kennedy, the President's sister most dedicated to this issue, was primarily on people with mental retardation rather than those with mental illness. But others in the Kennedy administration were eager for a major overhaul of the whole mental health system that would shift the focus of treatment from large state hospitals to flexible community mental health clinics. Stanley Yolles of the president's task force on mental health spoke confidently of such new community centers as making possible "for the mental hospital as it is now known to disappear from the scene within the next twenty-five years."[28]

According to a report of the surgeon general on mental health, "Enthusiasm for early interventions, developed by military mental health services during World War II, brought a new sense of optimism about treatment by the middle of the 20th century." As a result the concept of "community mental health" was born.[29] After some negotiation among competing interests, the Mental Retardation and Mental Health Centers Construction Act was passed in October 1963. This act provided three-year grants to aid states to set up community mental health centers. The authors of the act envisioned 2,000 such clinics developing over the next few years, but by 1980 only 754 had been built. What it meant to be cared for "in the community" was left vague and undefined, with the unwarranted assumption that most of those with mental illness who had lodged for years in hospitals had family to whom they could return. Expectations about the functions of community clinics were overloaded, with many seeing them as addressing all sorts of social ills. There also was no coordination between clinics and hospitals to see to it that those released from hospitals would be referred to the clinics. The result was that the clinics remained underfunded and unclearly defined, and often addressed issues of personality dysfunctions that had little to do with chronic mental illness. Psychiatric services expanded, but the most desperate of those with mental illness were little served by this expansion:

> Borrowing some ideas from the mental hygienists and capitalizing on the advent of new drugs for treating psychosis and depression, community mental health reformers argued that they could bring mental health services to the public in their communities. They suggested that long-term institutional care in mental hospitals had been neglectful, ineffective, even harmful. The joint policies of "community care" and "deinstitutionalization" led to dramatic declines in the length of hospital stay and the discharge of many patients from custodial care in hospitals. . . . The dual policies of community care and deinstitutionalization, however, were implemented without evidence of effectiveness of treatments and without a social welfare system attuned to the needs of hundreds of thousands of individuals with disabling mental illness. Housing, support services, community treatment approaches, vocational opportunities, and income supports for those unable to work were not universally available in the community. Neither was there a truly welcoming spirit of community support for "returning" mental patients. Many discharged mental patients found themselves in welfare and criminal justice institutions, as had their predecessors in earlier eras; some became homeless or lived in regimented residential (e.g., board and care) settings in the community.[30]

The quality of care within the community mental health care clinics seems to vary from locale to locale. While receiving federal funds, the clinics are maintained by states. According to the U.S. Department of

Health and Human Services–Substance Abuse and Mental Health Services Administration's National Health Information Center Web site,

> Because what is effective in one State may not be effective in another, the Community Mental Health Services Block Grant works in close collaboration with each State or Territory to develop and implement its own State Mental Health Plan for improving community-based services and reducing reliance on hospitalization.[31]

Our experience with community mental health clinics is limited to the one we had been told about before we arrived in Southern California in 2002. We immediately made contact with them on arrival, but found no receptivity to taking on David as a member. Two years ago we went back and found a new director who was more receptive. So David has had his psychiatrist and a social worker through this clinic, although he may soon change to the psychiatrist associated with his new residence. The clinic was bankrupt for several years, but now has received a new grant under new California moneys for mental illness and is anticipating some new development. We (my husband and I) have been asked to be on the board, which we are considering. This clinic seems to me to be weak and limited in its vision and resources. But it has provided a psychiatrist whom we know by name, whom we can talk to, even if briefly, and who gives us a copy of the medications he is prescribing, even though he sees David for only fifteen to twenty minutes every other month.

David also has been assigned a social worker through this clinic, a young Hispanic woman who seems to have little idea of what is appropriate for David. She tried to get him to go to a day program designed as a program for the elderly, which horrified him immediately when he saw the line of wheelchairs. She also suggested we look into an alternative housing venue, which turned out mostly for the wheelchair-bound elderly. After rejecting this option, David has now accepted it. In the first year she contacted David very infrequently and didn't seem to spend much time keeping track of him. However, in mid-December 2007 and again in mid-December 2008, she suddenly showed new interest in him and frantically called him to come in for a meeting with her. It was only after two years of this that I realized that this occasional interest had little to do with new initiatives on her part for him, but reflected the need to fill out end-of-the-year paperwork with each of her clients in order to keep the funding for her job.

The clinic has few work opportunities they can recommend for David, an issue of major interest to him, but about which he has no realistic understanding. Their housing manager is brusque and unhelpful in his attitude and seems to have nothing to offer that we don't already know. Six years ago, when I first contacted this clinic, they gave me a list of board-and-care homes in the Los Angeles county area, which I have used since in our efforts to find David housing. But this is now somewhat out of date. The clinic has said they are updating it, but they have not done so.

There is a young people's group that meets there that might actually be pretty good, but I have not succeeded in getting David to consider it, although I am still trying. David is very leery of anything that ties him either to the elderly or to groups he sees as demeaning his dignity. Groups of young people who have already bonded and where he feels himself the outsider are threatening to him. So this community mental health care clinic is a weak reed for us, but better than nothing.

The Advent of Medicare and Medicaid

In 1965, under the Johnson administration, another federal law would have a major impact on mental hospitals. This was the amendment to the Social Security Act of 1935, which set up Medicare and Medicaid. Medicare A covers hospital insurance for the indigent aged and Medicare B covers doctors' services. Medicaid gave medical assistance to the indigent, including those with mental illness. One result of this provision of federal funding for medical needs of those with mental illness was the rapid transfer of the huge numbers of the older segment of their group of people from hospitals to nursing homes. Nursing homes greatly expanded to meet this new role.

The numbers of chronic patients in mental hospitals fell by almost half in ten years, from 504,604 in 1962 to 274,837 in 1972 and to 55,000 by 2004. Many of these were elderly mentally ill patients, but some portion of those who were younger than sixty-five were also transferred from hospitals to nursing homes.[32] However, to describe this emptying of mental hospitals as "deinstitutionalization," as is commonly done, is inaccurate. What was actually happening was a lateral shift from one medical institution—the mental hospital, funded by the states—to another medical institution—the nursing home, funded by the federal government through Medicare and Medicaid. While the hospitals had had some aspirations of seeking cures for mental illness, the nursing home was purely custodial.

At the same time, mental hospitals, as well as psychiatric units of more general hospitals, changed their role. Admissions did not fall off but actually increased. From 1955 to 1970 admissions to mental hospitals doubled, from 178,003 to 384,511,[33] but these were now short-term stays, typically twenty-eight days at the most. Mental hospitals now became part of a revolving-door system in which those with an acute psychosis were admitted for brief observation, "stabilized" on psychiatric medications, and then released, presumably to some "community" agency, but in actuality often with little clear follow-up plan. The result was widespread homelessness of those with mental illness.

David has been a patient in a mental hospital and in the psychiatric wards of general hospitals since moving to California in July 2002. These are locked facilities, so David could not come and go freely, and we had to be checked in with elaborate security precautions. On entering the hospital, patients hand over shoelaces and sharp items, including pens, lest they be used to commit suicide or to injure someone else. Personal belongings are put in a box that is placed in hospital custody. Our experience is that these possessions are seldom returned in full when patients leave the hospital; David regularly lost the few possessions he had brought with him when he moved in.

David's hospital stays were generally two to three weeks in length, which had nothing to do with therapeutic need but everything to do with what state insurance would cover. It is assumed by mental health professionals that most people with mental illness can be treated by medication on an outpatient basis or in nursing homes. Consequently, long-term stays in hospitals are no longer necessary. While it is true that the development of psychiatric drugs did not "create" this emptying of mental hospitals, the drugs did contribute to redefining the role of mental hospitals in treating people with mental illness.

In 1980, at the end of the Carter administration, the Mental Health Systems Act was passed to try to strengthen the provisions of the Community Health Centers Act, but the provisions of this act were gutted by the Reagan administration, which sought to transfer authority for mental health back to the states from the federal government. At the same time the role of nursing homes in caring for those with mental illness grew. In 1985 there were 600,000 people with mental illness in nursing homes, more than the total of those in mental hospitals in 1955.[34] In our experience in Illinois, nursing homes were commonly used as a way of housing those with mental illness, sometimes with a separate floor for younger patients and sometimes simply mixed in with the elderly.

The next important piece of legislation that affected the housing of those with mental illness was the 1972 revision of the Social Security Act to allow people with mental illness to be defined as permanently disabled to receive Supplemental Security Income (SSI).[35] This monthly cash assistance (in 2008, $637 a month)[36] for a disabled person to meet the costs of food, shelter, and clothing, plus medical coverage from state Medicaid programs, made possible the creation of a new institution for housing those with mental illness: board-and-care homes, or PPHAs (Private Proprietary Homes for Adults). In order to make a profit, such homes need to minimize expenses. This means few and low-paid staff; bulk buying of cheap, starchy food; packing two to four residents per room; and providing no real services that might help a person go back to school or get a job.[37]

The Perennial Option of Last Resort: The Jail

From colonial times to the present, the jail has been the option of last resort for those with mental illness. In colonial America people with mental illness often were not distinguished from "rogues" and "vagabonds." The primary concern was public safety—preventing those not profitably employed and without settled residence from roaming around. As Albert Deutsch wrote, "Incarceration in jail was the common solution."[38] Jail did not necessarily mean an institution where those apprehended were kept long-term; instead, jail often meant gallows, pillories, and whipping posts where they were exhibited and punished.

Through the nineteenth and into the twentieth centuries, although state mental hospitals grew as the primary option for people with mental illness, they were sometimes hard to distinguish from prisons. The "insane," especially homeless persons who became involved in infractions of the law, such as vagrancy, drunkenness, and shoplifting, often found themselves in jail. The house of correction, or workhouse—a mix between a penal institution and a poorhouse, where those convicted of infractions were legally committed as prisoners—also included a certain number of people with mental illness.[39]

In the last half of the twentieth century, the jail returned as the major institution of last resort for those with mental illness, for much the same reason as in earlier times: because such people are homeless, unemployed, and get involved in minor infractions of the law. I do not speak here of special medical-penal institutions for the "criminally insane," that is, persons who commit major crimes and who are judged as insane and not competent to stand trial. These people are incarcerated in maximum security mental hospitals.[40] Rather, I speak here of a population whose brushes with the law come primarily from unemployment, homelessness, and efforts to survive on the street. Many are simply held for a period of time in jails until the judicial system finds other ways of disposing of them, but they never actually are convicted of a crime. Others are convicted of offenses, such as stealing or assault, and become mingled with the criminal population in prisons where they may or may not be recognized as having a mental illness that would cause them to be separated from other criminals and given psychiatric medications.

It is difficult to determine how many of America's prison population of more than two million have mental illness, because many of those convicted of crimes who may have mental illness are not diagnosed. Moreover, the very conditions of prisons may promote patterns of coping that would be judged in other settings as mental illness.[41] In some cases psychiatric medications may be overused in prisons to "calm" people who might not need them elsewhere. Fifty percent of the prisoners in Maine's Hancock County Jail are on some form of psychotropic medication, and the Los Angeles County Jail spends $10 million a year on psychiatric medication.[42]

One U.S. Department of Justice study estimates that about 10 percent or more than 200,000 prisoners in U.S. prisons have severe psychiatric disorders.[43] Another survey reports that more than half of all prisoners are mentally ill, with more women than men (73 percent of females and 55 percent of males in state prisons; 61 percent of females and 44 percent of males in federal prisons; and 73 percent of females and 63 percent of males in local jails).[44] The various types of prisons, from county jails to state and federal prisons, have become *de facto* the nation's largest institution for persons with mental illness with more residents in them than in all psychiatric hospitals put together.[45] As E. Fuller Torrey puts it: "Because of the failure of mental health professionals to provide medications and ensure aftercare for discharged patients, many individuals with schizophrenia undergo a revolving door of admissions and readmissions to hospitals, jails and public shelters."[46]

David had a minor brush with the law in his late teens, before being diagnosed with mental illness. As recounted in chapter 1, David was arrested by the Santa Cruz police for walking on a wall after he insulted them in Spanish. He was arrested for disorderly conduct and resisting arrest but was never formally charged. Had Herman and I not been so constantly vigilant about David's whereabouts and well-being over the last thirty years, he doubtless would have had more bouts of homelessness and hence brushes with the law.

Some American police departments have become more sophisticated in handling people with mental illness. Some police officers now receive special training in identifying such individuals and seeing that they are referred to psychiatric hospitals.[47] On one of David's "long walks" in Los Angeles, he was apprehended by the Redondo Beach police when he was rifling through a garbage dumpster for food. He was given care for his bleeding feet and conveyed to the psychiatric ward of a local hospital without being incarcerated in a jail. His good treatment probably owed something to the fact that he is white and relatively "middle-class" looking. The police also have an interest in not filling their jails with noncriminal vagrants with mental illness.

Patients' Rights

Some attention should be given to the subject of the rights of those with mental illness, since this has been the subject of controversy in recent writings. Rael Isaac and Virginia Armat, in their 1990 book, *Madness in the Streets: How Psychiatry and the Law Abandoned the Mentally Ill*,[48] spend three chapters condemning the "mental health bar" (legal defenders of patients' rights) for allowing people with mental illness to "die with their rights on"; that is, become abandoned and homeless in the streets through shortsighted defenses of their rights to refuse admission to hospitals and to refuse treatment.

The question of the legal rights of those with mental illness is not a new one in American society. Until the mid-nineteenth century, commitment of the "insane" was presumed to be the right of the family and public authorities without any public inquiry. However, the fear of wrongful commitment of the sane by a malicious family member or by business associates was a theme of popular culture.[49] This issue was highlighted by the case of Mrs. E. P. W. Packard, who was committed by her husband to an insane asylum in Illinois in 1860. She gained her freedom three years later and thereafter engaged in a crusade across America to get states to pass laws that would prevent commitment of a person to an insane asylum simply on the grounds of that individual's expressions of personal opinions.[50] At that time Illinois law allowed married women or children to be committed to an insane asylum by their husband, father, or guardian, "without the evidence of insanity required in other cases."

As a result of this and other challenges, many states passed laws making the process of commitment more rigorous. There had to be a formal petition by a family member, friend, or public official. Proof of insanity had to be certified by a physician, and sometimes two. There had to be a public hearing and formal commitment order, and a person "charged" with insanity could demand a trial by jury. Laws were developed to allow people to voluntarily commit themselves, stipulating that if they asked for a release, it must be granted within a few weeks. But generally, the superintendent of the hospital had absolute discretion on the decision to release a person when he (and it was always a "he" in these years) was satisfied that the person was sufficiently cured. Some states provided for a parole system where a released person was supervised by a social worker or psychiatrist for some time after release.[51]

There was little attention to questions of informed consent or right to refuse treatment in the nineteenth to mid-twentieth centuries. It was common in hospitals to force-feed food or medication if patients refused it. In the 1960s the mental hospital, and especially the practice of electroshock and psychosurgery, was scandalized by stories of patients beings forcibly dragged by nurses to have teeth and organs removed in Henry Cotton's New Jersey State Hospital, or being forced to submit to electroshock or lobotomy without their consent, as was the case in various mental hospitals. Thus, patients' rights became a major issue of the reform movement of that time. Several lawyers specialized in securing the legal rights of mental patients.[52]

States and the federal government subsequently have passed laws clarifying these rights. According to California law, "persons with mental illness have the same legal rights and responsibilities guaranteed by the Federal Constitution and laws and the laws of California, unless specifically limited by Federal or state law or regulations."[53] These rights include the right to "dignity, privacy and humane care," to physical exercise and social interaction, and to be free of hazardous procedures. When in a psychiatric facility, one has a right to wear one's own clothing, keep personal possessions, have individual storage space for one's use, see visitors every day, have reasonable access to phones both to make and receive calls, have letter writing material and stamps, and have the right to send and receive unopened correspondence."

Key rights in terms of psychiatric treatment are "the right to give or withhold informed consent to medical and psychiatric treatment, including the right to refuse antipsychotic medication, unless specific emergency criteria are met or there has been a judicial determination of incapacity," "the right to participate in the development of individualized treatment and services planning," "the right to refuse psychosurgery," "the right to confidentiality," "the right to inspect and copy the medical record, unless specific criteria are met," "the right to have family and friends notified of certain treatment with patient's permission," and "the right to an aftercare plan."[54]

These legal rights seem to me to be reasonable, and, if properly interpreted in practice, they should avoid forced treatment that a person doesn't want while also keeping a clearly psychotic person from languishing in the streets untreated. The problem, as in all laws, is how such laws are actually administered and enforced. Our experience with David is that he has not really been consulted about whether he wants to be taken to a mental hospital. He simply is put in an ambulance and taken there, where, upon arrival is met with the quick formality of being asked to sign in. Medications have been administered to him without asking his consent or even explaining to him what they are.

To really inform him about how the medications (supposedly) work and to involve him in planning his own treatment would be a big step forward, but this is not done. Most annoying to us as parent-advocates is how mental hospitals and wards of hospitals have several times refused to tell us on the grounds of "confidentiality" whether David was actually there or not, or when he was released. Thus, David's "right" to confidentiality is used to block another of his "rights": namely, information given to family and friends. Since his father is his "conservator," he also has a "right" to this information.

Recovery or Maintenance?

What have we as a society lost in terms of a vision of what a curative environment might look like? In many ways the "moral treatment" of the York Retreat and like reform movements of the early nineteenth century still offer a better vision of what a curative environment might be like than anything that has developed since, either in the large mental hospital or in the current array of options (jail, homelessness and homeless shelters, board-and-care homes, nursing homes, and community mental health clinics).

What the "moral treatment" movement grasped most clearly was that recovery is about loving relationships for each person as an individual and a sense of affirmation of each person as a human with the potential for what Quakers would call the "inner light," or what Christians have traditionally called "the image of God." They also understood that idleness was bad for people's mental health or, conversely, that for persons to recover they need stimulating activities—work, recreation, and education. Such activities need to be attractive and meaningful, not used punitively, as they once were in the mental hospital.

Gardening, sewing circles, cooking, and a print shop where patients could publish their writing were among the options at the York Retreat. Recreation was varied, but often included sports teams. Men formed cricket teams (in England) or football clubs (in the United States). Tennis, croquet, and other team games were available for women. Music groups formed and played concerts. Even in U.S. mental hospitals, there were worship groups that included active choirs. Anton Boisen, in his work as a chaplain at Worcester and Elgin state mental hospitals in the 1920s to the 1950s, developed a worship book designed for those in mental hospitals and organized vested choirs of the patients, which he saw as having significant therapeutic value.[55] Plays were not only read, but drama groups were formed to put them on. In short, there were adult activities, not mindless diversion that treated those with mental illness as either children with learning disabilities or persons with senility.

In my view, meaningful and stimulating work, recreation, and education are still vital for a curative environment—that is, an environment where one hopes for recovery and does not simply aim at maintenance. The problem with today's options for persons with mental illness is not, first of all, lack of resources, but most of all lack of vision. It is a system that aims not at recovery but only at maintenance, with keeping people dependent and passive.

6

What Would We Do if We Really Cared?

The mental health resources available to us in the Pomona Valley area of Southern California are woefully inadequate. They express *de facto* a limited purpose aimed at warehousing and maintenance of those with mental illness, not hope, recovery, and a fuller life. Yet the United States and many other countries are full of projects that understand what is needed. These projects have been founded by visionary people who have dedicated themselves to making a difference for people with mental illness, not just making a living off them.

We have first-hand experience with four such projects, and recently have discovered and personally investigated another. Although its location makes it unavailable to David at the moment, the fifth project provides a model that might be adapted to our area. The following is a discussion of these five models and an analysis of why they work. All offer components in keeping with the fuller vision and practice that is needed in caring for people with mental illness.

Duck Island, Maine

Great Duck Island is a small island 1.5 miles long and a half mile wide in the Gulf of Maine. In 1890 a lighthouse was established there, and for years the Coast Guard had a station on the island. In 1963 Boston psychotherapist George Cloutier bought most of the island. He constructed an airstrip so he could fly a small plane there and ran a psychiatric clinic and intentional community from 1970 to 1979 (when it closed), housed in a geodesic dome and a collection of small cabins constructed in the style of yurts.

David resided in this therapeutic community in the summer of 1979, together with about nineteen other young people. He thrived there and remembers it as one of his best experiences. Cloutier ran it mostly by himself with few other staff members. Cloutier did not believe in psychiatric medication, and David went off medications that summer. Although he believes it took him much of the summer to "recover" from taking medication, he remembers feeling better there than when he was on meds. This experience remains a model for him of an active, medication-free life.

Day-to-day life on the island that summer entailed vigorous communal work. All supplies were brought over from the mainland by boat. David helped load the boat in high surf, row to the island, and unload the supplies. He also participated in collective food preparation and cleanup and maintenance of the community. He spent a lot of time walking around the island, down to the lighthouse and Coast Guard station and back, and what he saw is included in some of his best poetry. He left these writings in the main room when he left, which he still regrets. It is hard to imagine what would have happened to David had the community been open longer and David had stayed there through the winter.

Gould Farm, Massachusetts

Gould Farm is one of the longest standing, best organized, and most comprehensive therapeutic communities and programs in the country. It was started in 1913 by William J. and Agnes Gould, who purchased a 650-acre farm and adjacent forestland in the Berkshire Mountains of western Massachusetts and began to invite guests, some of them with physical and emotional challenges, to live with them. William Gould died in 1925 fighting a forest fire, and Agnes Gould set up the farm as a nonprofit trust in 1929. The farm continues to operate as a nonprofit trust and accepts no insurance, state, or federal monies. Guests pay for their stay there on a sliding scale according to their ability to pay. Full payment is $325 a day ($10,000 a month or $120,000 a year).

The Gould Farm community consists of a maximum of forty-three guests with diagnosed mental illness such as schizophrenia, bipolar or schizoaffective disorders, or major depression, together with volunteers and staff, many of whom live on the farm with their families. Most guests are in their twenties and early thirties, although a few are older. Three residential houses provide private rooms for the guests with a shared living room, a kitchenette, and bathrooms. Each of the three houses has a residential advisor who works with an overall clinical director. All the guests have household chores to perform, along with regular meetings with a therapist to develop living skills and to discuss social relations. It is assumed that most guests are taking psychiatric medication.

In addition to household chores, all the guests are part of a work team that maintains the farm as a commercial enterprise and a partly self-sustaining community. The workday is six hours, morning and afternoon, with lunch break. Everyone on a work team is expected to be at work on time. After breakfast (7:30–8 a.m.), the day starts with a brief community meeting from 8:05 to 8:20. The workday starts promptly at 8:30 and goes to 11:30. After an hour-long lunch at noon, work resumes from 1 to 4 p.m. Then there is free time, followed by dinner and optional evening activities.

There are seven work teams. The farm team cares for the dairy and beef cattle and pigs and hens, collects and cleans eggs, harvests hay, repairs fences and farm equipment, and works in the dairy barn. The garden team grows and harvests a large variety of organic vegetables. This means starting the seeds in the greenhouse, preparing the fields for planting, transferring the seedlings to the fields, tending them through the growing season, watering, weeding, debugging them, and finally harvesting the vegetables that are used for the daily meals of the community. In addition, the vegetables are used at the farm's roadside café and are sold to the public through the farm's store.

A forestry and grounds team tends the woodlands, trails, and grounds, as well as indoor common living areas. They mow the lawns, do seasonal landscaping, keep trails open, cut wood for each of the houses, tap the maple trees to produce maple syrup, and keep the tools in repair. The harvest barn team operates a major commercial enterprise of the farm. The barn houses a commercial kitchen that processes a variety of foods including cheese, butter, maple syrup, and baked goods, which are marketed both to those who come to the barn to shop and also through a mail-order service. The office that manages these commercial enterprises is also located in the harvest barn.

The kitchen team prepares three meals a day for about a hundred people including the guests, volunteers, and the staff and their families. Members of the kitchen team work under a kitchen manager, but they also are encouraged to try out their own recipes. They are responsible for cleanup after meals. The maintenance team takes care of the thirty-five buildings on campus—guest residences, staff houses, repair shops, and the large farmhouse that is the administrative and clinical headquarters and the place for community meetings. This means doing needed repairs of the buildings and furniture, plumbing, electrical work, and painting.

Gould Farm also runs a roadside café and store, where people can enjoy breakfast or lunch with fresh farm vegetables and eggs and home-made butter and maple syrup. The café is famous for its pancakes, and the pancake mix is also sold through the store and the mail-order service. Guests can work there, preparing and serving the food, handling the cash and credit card payments, ordering and stocking merchandise, and generally learning the skills of managing a restaurant and small store.

Although guests used to be able to stay at Gould Farm indefinitely, in 1999 it was decided to accept guests for a maximum of three years. Most stay less. They then can move on to a transitional program in Medford, Massachusetts, near Boston. A residence provides transitional housing for these graduated guests who by now are expected to self-administer their medications, manage daily living skills, and engage in vocational training, education, and volunteer work or a paid job. This transitional housing then prepares people to move into their own apartments or houses when they are able to fully care for themselves, although still with some support from a network of supportive friends, therapists, and counselors. After a year of independent living, a former guest can apply to return to the farm as a volunteer worker.

Gould Farm has a comprehensive vision and program designed to move people with mental illness from dependence to autonomy and independent living through hope, empowerment, and learned basic living and work skills. Both residential living and the work teams are integral to a therapeutic process of enabling people to learn through experience to work together and function personally and socially as an adult, even while still needing to cope with elements of continued mental illness that may require taking medication.[1]

Gould Farm presently caters to a small and discrete number of guests. It has a large number of highly motivated staff who work intensively with each individual, both as therapists and as directors of work teams. The costs are high, and since the farm does not accept insurance or state funds, most of this must come from the individual or the individual's family. It demands a high level of readiness to accept a disciplined routine. David failed there after a few months in the mid-1980s because he was not ready to accept the discipline. Also, we did not have the money to keep him there much longer.

It would be easy to dismiss Gould Farm as an option available only to the wealthy and assume it could not be adapted to serve poorer people. But this is not necessarily the case. The same Supplemental Security Income (SSI) funds from the federal government and state mental health and Medicare funding, together with other kinds of state and county grants, that fund for-profit board-and-care homes could fund a better-quality therapeutic community. What it would take are visionary staff members who are willing to put in more intensive time with a group of twenty to forty residents; a bit of land where food might be grown or other productive activities organized—such as a print shop; and the effort to organize the residents to do the work of community maintenance together.

Kahumana, Hawaii

Kahumana is a much more informal operation than Gould Farm. It has a little more than twenty-year history as a therapeutic community. Kahumana was started by a group of people from different religious backgrounds—an Eastern rite priest, a Catholic nun trained as a psychotherapist, and some people from the Anthroposophical tradition who were working together with homeless persons with mental illness in Honolulu. They decided in the mid-1980s to create a rural community in the Waianae area of Oahu, Hawaii, to care for people with mental illness. The founders moved to the site with their families, so it also became their residence.

Kahumana features organic food raised onsite and a concern for healthy eating. It has space for sixteen residents with retardation or emotional or physical illness. Work is available by caring for the grounds or in food production and preparation. David was given the job of taking care of the chickens. He also helped in the orchards. The Kahumana staff was pleased that David was a willing worker, unlike (they told me) some of the other residents who preferred to stay in their rooms and watch television. But work was much more of an individual choice; there was nothing like the organized work teams and the set workday of Gould Farm.

There were also recreational activities. David was enrolled in a tennis program at a nearby club and worked with a horse-riding project, but such activities proved transitory. Kahumana is walking distance to a beautiful swimming beach, and David enjoyed such walks and swims. The Kahumana Web site advertises arts and crafts classes, gardening, landscaping, food production, household maintenance, and kitchen assistance.[2] Kahumana holds out a vision of a healing landscape and has constructed a labyrinth and water gardens to express this. David did well there for a year, less well the second year, and then was thrown out for hitting someone. It too was becoming prohibitively expensive for us.

Thresholds, Illinois

Thresholds is a network of therapeutic services in Chicago organized to serve large numbers of those with mental illness of all economic classes, but particularly those with few resources. It is funded by private payment, insurance, and state funds through the Illinois Department of Mental Health, the Illinois Department of Rehabilitation Services, and the Illinois Department of Children and Family Services. Medicaid and SSI are also used for residential programs and medical services, so Thresholds can offer its many clients free or affordable services. It presently serves about 6,000 people with mental illness annually.[3]

The people served by Thresholds are called "members"—members of a community, a network, and a movement. Introduction to membership in the Threshold community starts at the drop-in center housed in a large former mansion near downtown Chicago. There persons with mental illness can be taken in and incorporated both into support groups and into light maintenance work. Beginning members are put in work teams that clean the building and help prepare the nourishing meals that are served each day. Some with more advanced skills might do some of the clerical work and receive members in the reception area.

Members can also be incorporated into "clubhouses," or support groups, near where they live, where they come together to socialize and develop supportive friendships. Thresholds also runs outreach programs to the homeless and to those in the jails. Thresholds staff go out to find people with mental illness who are living in the streets or who are using homeless shelters for a bed and an evening meal. They work with the courts to contact those who have fallen afoul of the law due to minor offenses. Through their bridge program, they visit people in their homes to find out what is happening to them. These outreach programs seek to find people with mental illness, people who are getting lost, and bring them into programs.

Once a member proves willing and able to work with a group through the drop-in center, Thresholds has a number of services to offer him or her. One of these is residential services. Thresholds runs seventy-five residences including supervised group homes, single rooms in a former hotel (single room occupancy or SRO) run by Thresholds as a supportive housing setting, and independent apartments. All have various levels of supportive services intended to help residents manage basic living skills, food preparation, money management, and community relations.

Thresholds also runs a mothers' program that helps suffering mothers suggering from mental illness with parenting skills and support and provides residence in group homes designed for members with small children.

Thresholds has an educational program that helps members finish high school and move on to college or to vocational training. A number of sites around the city offer classes for members to gain basic educational skills in math, reading, writing, and computer literacy in order to get their GED or high school equivalency certificate and prepare to enter college classes. There is also a scholarship program to help pay for college classes.

The vocational program at Thresholds enables people to prepare to enter the job market and to find a job placement. It funds a number of rehabilitation industries where a person can learn to work in a paying job run by Thresholds itself. This includes a laser cartridge manufacturing business, an assembly and packaging business, a cleaning service, a copying service, and a florist service. All of these businesses have a well-established clientele. The cartridge manufacturing business sells to the U.S. Postal Service, the Department of Defense, and Office Depot. Clients of the packaging business include the LaSalle Bank in Chicago, and clients of the cleaning service include the University of Illinois in Chicago. The florist does flower arrangements for weddings, funerals, and special events.

An extensive "expressive arts" program operates though Thresholds' various centers. This includes crafts and sculpture sold at fairs, gardening and flower arranging, dance classes and training of dance therapists, theatre programs, newspapers and writing classes, and music. The theatre arts program connects members with the large network of independent theatres in Chicago, both to learn skills and to participate in putting on shows. Musical training includes a music camp where members participate in piano, guitar, songwriting, and instrument-creating workshops and create CDs of their music.

Thresholds has the most extensive and comprehensive set of services for people with mental illness in the country. No one is turned away for lack of funds. A person just needs to get past the door, settle in to a support group, and gain the motivation to commit himself or herself to work with a program. Unfortunately, David was not able to do that. He dropped out on the first try in 1982, partly due to an unwillingness to take medications, and never got past the door of the drop-in center on the second try fourteen years later. Thresholds might have tried harder to get him involved, but this was mostly David's failure. To quote an old adage, "You can lead a horse to water, but you can't make him drink."

The most fundamental problem for the recovery of people with mental illness is not, first of all, what array of services a good program offers or should offer, but how to motivate people to make the first steps to really try to better themselves, particularly people like David, who has adapted himself to a low level of functioning and is resistant to entering a new situation where he fears he might not be accepted. Reawakening hope is the first step. It is this factor that has been clearly recognized by an innovative program in Long Beach, California: MHA Village.

MHA Village, California

MHA Village is an integrated-services center that helps people with mental illnesses recover and become able to live and work within their communities. It does not own residences but helps people find their own housing and be able to do what is needed to function in this housing. The Village also puts the major focus on helping people get a job and recover the self-esteem of employment, even if this is only part-time. It has supportive counseling that includes medication, but it views medication as an adjunct to learning how to manage one's own life and health, freeing oneself from dependence on a mental health system based on maintenance, rather than "getting a life." Medication is negotiated between the psychiatrist and the person. The psychiatrist presents several options of medications and explains their effects and allows the person to decide what he or she will take.

MHA Village is located in downtown Long Beach, California, and was started in 1990 by a group of people concerned about the fragmentation of services to people with mental illness that disconnected the different aspects of what they needed. Medical services seldom were related to housing needs, and neither the clinics that prescribed medications nor board-and-care housing had any opportunities for employment. Hospitals, in turn, did not communicate with clinics. Village founders sought to bring these various services together at one counseling center.

MHA Village presently serves about 500 people who are seen as members of a community, not as clients or patients. It is based in a multistoried building in downtown Long Beach, but the staff does not stay isolated in this building. Much of their time is engaged in supporting their members as they make their way into new lives in the community Outreach teams contact homeless people to establish trusting relationships with them and encourage them to come to the center for services.

Mark Ragins, resident psychiatrist at the Village, sees the vision of the Village as one that was a transformative journey for himself, as it is for those he serves. In order to arrive at this vision, he had to unlearn much of the way he was taught to view and treat people with mental illness by his psychiatric education:

> As a psychiatrist I had been taught to manage serious mental illness with a set of assumptions that if articulated would sound something like this: "People with chronic mental illness are permanently disabled. Medicate them and forget them. They are weak and need to be taken care of. They can't hold down jobs. They have no significant role to play in society. The possibility of them having a meaningful life is slight. Their prognosis is hopeless."[4]

For Ragins to discover the vision of recovery as the goal of services to those with mental illness was like a conversion experience. He realized that he had been confusing recovery and cure. A person with a major mental illness may never be cured in the sense that all symptoms disappear, but he or she can learn to manage this illness and get on with life in ways that engage normal activities of independent living, such as resuming one's education, getting a job, and even raising a family.

For Ragins, recovery from mental illness goes through four stages. The first is hope. A person with mental illness needs to shake off passivity and hopelessness, which is not only a "negative symptom" of the disease but also is inculcated through the mental "health" system itself, through its doctors and its system of "treatment." Hope means discovering an idea of something one wants to do to make a better life for oneself, even if it is only a small step, like dressing, keeping clean, and looking better. Hope can expand in larger and larger visions, but it often begins with small decisions to do something for oneself. Hope is what gives a person energy for new life.

With the birth of hope, even a small hope, comes the need for empowerment. This is the second stage. The Village seeks to empower people by giving them access to information and opportunities and, above all, by supporting them to take risks and to begin to believe that they have the capacity to do something more than they are presently doing. Taking risks is usually seen as something to be avoided by people with mental illness, since it causes stress that may result in a "relapse." But any venture for new life is risky and stressful. Stress itself is a manifestation of being alive. To live totally without stress is to be dead.

So when someone begins to formulate an idea of something he or she wants to do, the Village philosophy is to encourage that person to try it and not wait to feel "ready," for one can never become ready except by trying. If helped to see the failure as a learning experience, to evaluate what caused the failure and try again. The Village never abandons people who fail, even if they become psychotic and create major disasters. Once a person is a member, the staff of the Village has a permanent commitment to that person and will stick with him or her through continual failures, helping the individual to learn from experience and try again, hopefully in a new and better way.

This is in dramatic contrast to most mental health services, whose policy is to "throw" the person out after a few failures have indicated that the individual is not "working out." How would David's life been different if he had not spent so much of it being "thrown out" of various programs and housing for failures, instead of being encouraged to learn from the failure and try again? As Ragins put it: "It is our job [as staff at the Village] to keep hope alive and support our members through ongoing stress and risk-taking, failures and successes as they recover."[5]

The third stage of recovery for Ragins is self-responsibility. This stage grows out of hope and empowerment as the person begins to take more and more responsibility for his or her own life. This means breaking with patterns of dependency and getting over blaming other people or oneself for mistakes and failures. Again, this is ongoing process. One begins to take more responsibility for self-care, for taking care of one's own health. As mentioned before, Ragins as a psychiatrist does not just prescribe medication, but also consults with the person about the options and discusses the side effects. The person then decides which medication to try, and in what amount, and takes responsibility for taking the meds within his or her overall life plan. Taking psychiatric medication is no longer isolated from deciding to get up in the morning, get dressed, have breakfast, and get out in time to a job or other activity.

The fourth stage to recovery is to find a meaningful role in life. This does not necessarily mean becoming a highly paid professional. It means discarding the role of a chronic mental patient and finding a role that is meaningful and fulfilling. This might mean finding a place as a server in soup kitchen for homeless people and becoming the person who makes the soup every day. It means finding something you can do fairly well and where you can have a meaningful place within a community of friends or family. It means what the Village calls "getting a life."

The Village staff works with people on a variety of skills that helps them toward this goal of recovery. Being able to get a job is a central part of their agenda, since they believe that having paid work is what most defines an autonomous adult in U.S. society. It is hard for anyone to have self-esteem if they do not have a job. MHA Village starts by offering many jobs within the operation of the Village itself. Members run the convenience store, a café, and a savings bank in the Village, and people can start getting jobs through these activities. Many members are also employed as staff in the Village, doing all sorts of work, including being counselors. There are also many jobs in the community, starting with day labor, that Village staff can offer members.

Getting one's own apartment is an important goal, and the Village runs a whole array of support services to help people find apartments, do what is necessary to keep them, and live in them in a self-supporting way. Some people discover they can go back to school, earn a degree, and get a well-paying job. But for many, the jobs are small and not well-paying. Members have to juggle the satisfaction of earning income with the threat of losing their Social Security benefits. The way these benefits are defined by the government as conditioned by a state of permanent "disability" is a major impediment to the kind of recovery and self-responsibility the Village defines as its goal, so the staff has to work around these contradictions.[6]

But the core of success in the process of recovery, for Ragins, is not how high the external social status someone might achieve. Recovery is an inner process within the self by which a person moves from despondency and hopelessness to hope, from the learned role of the dependent mental patient to becoming a person with some sense of one's value, one's capacity to work, and one's ability to have friendships and take responsibility for oneself and care for others. Recovery, finally, is the process of becoming a self-actualizing person in relationships.

Imagining a Better System

Duck Island, Gould Farm, Kahumana, Thresholds, and MHA Village each have key components of what is necessary to build a better system. First and most important is work. No one is allowed simply to be a passive recipient of services. Chores to maintain the community are the first line of work. People are incorporated into cleaning buildings, preparing and cleaning up after meals, caring for the grounds, and taking care of one's own room, if there are residences. This is in marked contrast with most board-and-care homes, where all the maintenance work is done for the residents, and the residents live in total idleness. Secondly, people are incorporated into gaining skills for paid work, sometimes starting at the center itself, such as helping run the office. But then they are moved into paid work in enterprises that the network supervises and sustains.

Education is also important in helping people recover. This does not mean finger painting and bingo; rather, it means classes that really help people move on to finish high school and begin college or education for further employable skills. Recreation should also be a part of a good program, but that recreation should be useful for health and for building community, such as basketball teams or yoga classes. People are not allowed to become couch potatoes watching TV all day. Thresholds differs from MHA Village in an important way in that the full range of its programs is integrated into and managed within its system, while the Village owns little beside its coordinating center. The Village's approach is to integrate people into housing, work, and programs within the larger society, not to run them itself.

The limitation of the five programs discussed here is that they are unique, exceptional efforts by a particular visionary individual or group of people who build a program in a particular area, which doesn't change the rest of the mental health system in the county, state, or nation. Two of the cases, Gould Farm and Kahumana, are too expensive for all but the rich. Duck Island was an experiment by one individual that was not sustained. The two other cases, Thresholds and MHA Village, are more integrated into the local mental health system and generally affordable by everyone, particularly those with mental illness who lack economic resources and are dependent on state and federal funding.

My vision is for a better mental health system, a system whose goal is recovery. My vision would build especially on Thresholds and MHA Village, with some insights from the other three programs, to imagine how existing institutions that care for people with mental illness—the hospital, the board-and-care home, and the community mental health clinic—could be brought into better integration. I do not address the nursing home, which should not be used for mental patients except for brief recuperations from a physical injury. Nursing homes also need to be radically rethought as creative communities where ill or elderly people can participate in a meaningful way, but that is not a subject for this book.[7] David's present residency in a quasi-nursing home facility is a problem that makes his long-term stay there questionable.

The relation of the hospital, the board-and-care home, and the community mental health clinic needs to be integrated in real interconnection and their roles radically reconceived to aim at recovery, not just maintenance. It seems to me that the best integration should be at the county level, with a supervisory and funding role for the state, as well as funding from the federal level. Each county should have an integrated system of mental health services that interconnects housing, community clinics, and hospitals. Perhaps there should be a supervisory agency lodged at the county level that keeps track of all the mental patients who have come under the care of the system and that sees that each person is receiving the services he or she needs.

The Role of Mental Health Professionals

As is done in the Hawaii system, which provides for a permanent social worker for each person (although on the state level), each person should be assigned a social worker who continues to follow-up with him or her as long as the individual is in the county system, whether in a hospital, a board-and-care home, or in independent living. These social workers could be based at community clinics, but they would continue to relate to the person even if he or she moves to different situations, becomes homeless, or is in jail. Thus, the relation of persons with mental illness and their social workers would have some stability and permanence.

This need not be set in stone. There could be some possibility of changing the social worker, if the person is not getting on well with his or her social worker or has moved to a different part of the county not readily accessible to the clinic. But this needs to take place through consultation with the person and between the former and new social workers so there is full exchange of information. The county system should know who the social worker is for each person under its care.

The psychiatric hospital is there for crisis situations of violent and chaotic breakdown. It should be the place where there is a comprehensive evaluation, not simply of what medications might be appropriate but including the whole profile of the person's history, skills, and needs. The hospital should coordinate with the county office that keeps track of all the persons receiving services in the county system. Hospitalization would be followed by housing placement and the assignment of a social worker to the person, based at the community clinic closest to the housing. The person then would see his or her social worker and connect with a personal psychiatrist through the local clinic.

The psychiatrist is expected to receive a full profile of the person's life history, not simply what medications have been assigned. He or she should establish a meaningful communication with the person about the person's experience with medication and his or her recovery plans. This would mean meeting for at least half an hour to an hour each month, not fifteen minutes every other month. The psychiatrist should explain to the person the options for medication and the effects of different medications. The psychiatrist and the person should negotiate some decisions about this together, rather than the psychiatrist imposing a particular battery of medication without discussion.

It is essential that the psychiatrist establish a real relation with the person that makes possible a conversation about the person's experiences, needs, and wants. This is not a question of offering some set system of "talk therapy," but of a relationship of trust. The person should be able to discuss frankly with the psychiatrist his or her experience of the effects of the medication, including the option of rejection of medication. If the person being counseled doesn't trust the psychiatrist as someone he or she can talk to about this and other matters, this psychiatrist has failed to establish the basic conditions of relationship to that person. This seems to me to be a basic problem with the relationship between persons afflicted with mental illness and the current psychiatric profession. Clearly, David sees psychiatrists simply as pill-pushers, not people he can trust with discussion of his real experiences.

The person would also connect with the social worker on at least a monthly basis. But this should be a more flexible and active presence. The social worker should sometimes meet with the person at his or her housing and go out for coffee and conversation. The social worker should be available to intervene when there is some crisis, perhaps counseling the person several days in succession. The social worker is in charge of helping the person with housing, job placements, educational options, and other forms of social outreach. Finally, the psychiatrist and the social worker should be in communication with each other on the overall services needed, the decisions made, and the recovery plan.

Appropriate Living Arrangements

The housing system for persons needing mental health services should be radically redeveloped into a coordinated network, with each housing group held to certain standards and ways of operating. In order to receive federal and state aid, each housing group needs to adhere to these standards. While for-profit housing groups could still develop outside this network, they would not receive state and federal aid. This would ensure that most of such housing groups would become a part of the network and adhere to its standards. This housing system should function on two levels—one level that is more of a full-service housing community and a second level of more independent living apartments that are supervised regularly.

The full-service group-living facility would house somewhere between ten and twenty persons "in recovery," as well as some resident staff. The staff would include someone able to manage the facility economically and legally. Day-to-day medications, as agreed upon by the psychiatrist and the resident, would be distributed by a staff member at the housing facility. But much more of the work of the facility should be done by the residents themselves. Each resident should have his or her own private room and be responsible for cleaning and keeping it in order.

In the various board-and-care homes in which he has lived, David has sometimes had a private room and sometimes shared a room with a roommate. He actually has seemed to have done better with a roommate. David sometimes becomes isolated and even acts out destructively in a private room, while having a roommate seems to give him some built-in controls and relationships. But I think that was because there were no community activities or expectations of care for his room. Also, with such community activities and expectations, I believe it is best if individuals have private space where they can keep their possessions.

The facility should have bathrooms for each group of four rooms, lounges where small groups can gather, class and craft rooms, a group meeting room large enough in which the whole community might gather (this could be the dining room), some recreation facilities (such as a basketball court), a kitchen, a dining room, and a laundry. Garden space for growing food and flowers is also recommended.

Meaningful Work

All residents should be expected to clean their own rooms and make their beds regularly, rather than relying on employed cleaning people to clean the rooms. There could be a rotation of those in each four-room group responsible for cleaning the bathroom. Someone would need to supervise all this to be sure that linens are handed out and collected and cleaning tools circulated. This could become a paid job for one of the residents. Residents would also be assigned to teams that would help clean the grounds and prepare and clean up after meals, with a paid coordinator of these services who could also be a resident. Gardening could be a recreational activity for those interested. Weekly meetings would be held to assign chores and discuss community work. This means that the members of the community have to participate in the chores of daily life, as they would if they had their own home, rather than having this work done for them in a way that enforces passive dependence.

In addition, each person would begin to be integrated into a larger system of paid work. This might start with being employed within the housing community itself as coordinator of work groups or doing some office work or supervising the laundry or other task. But the county, together with the network of local clinics, should have a number of supervised work sites, partnering with organizations such as the local park service (picking up trash, raking leaves), forest service (clearing trails in local mountains), manufacturing companies (packaging goods), and local schools (buildings and grounds work). Perhaps, like the WPA jobs projects of the Great Depression, a system of public-works jobs could be developed, based at the county level. Each person would receive some training to begin participating at a supervised work site. Individuals would receive at least minimum wage for this work.

Payment for such work would involve adjusting the federal rules about how much income a person could earn while continuing to receive SSI or other such state and federal funds. This would require some new federal and state legislation. The laws about paid employment of those on state and federal aid would have to be revised to allow people to continue to receive such aid on a sliding scale up to the point where they can really become self-sustaining for at least their housing (but still allowing for funds for medical needs). As persons become integrated into more full-time paid work, they also need to have regular counseling in managing their money, keeping a checkbook, and maintaining a bank account.

The goal is to help people develop some employable job skills that enable them to move on toward economic independence. As people become more independent, they also can move from the full-service communal housing to independent apartments, where they do their own shopping, cooking, and cleaning, but are still connected with a housing supervisor. Each person's social worker could also help with problems of daily functioning.

Educational Opportunities

Educational opportunities could be offered on the level of communal housing, through the community mental health clinics, or through city or county adult education programs, but in ways that support the person venturing into renewed education to connect with meaningful goals, such as finishing a GED, going to college, or completing professional training. The network of communities could also offer recreational and cultural opportunities, such as dance or yoga classes, team sports, choirs, and the like. The clinic or housing group might also relate to local YMCAs and YWCAs to offer swimming and recreational programs. The "day program," of infantile activities, would be abolished, but there would still be the opportunity to form groups for mutual support and socializing. These activities would seek to employ persons with mental illness, rather than only outside staff, thus getting such persons to take responsibility for activities and gaining skills in doing so.

Overcoming Obstacles through Advocacy and Support

Such an integrated plan of mental health services that connects hospitals, local mental health clinics, housing, employment, and education would need to be worked out in much greater detail than the above sketch. Problems of legal, economic, and social relationships need to be discussed in detail by those with expertise in these areas. Some experimental efforts should be tested by one or more county systems before being recommended more widely. MHA Village already represents one such venture through the Mental Health Association of Los Angeles County. The key is a commitment to recovery, rather than simply maintenance.

This brief sketch of what a better system would look like does not convey the urgency of the present crisis situation, as well as the terrible frustration that those working with it experience. Dick Bunce, activist with the Los Angeles County mental health system, on reviewing this chapter, wrote the following comment:

> I agree with your descriptions of the role of psychiatrist and social worker. Yet the practical constraints are overwhelming—the need for a vast amount of retraining and the need for an enormous increase in provider services. Huge caseloads and the paucity of housing, jobs and other services crush the best intentions of providers within a fortnight. . . . Yet, except for MHSA [Mental Health Services Administration], funding trends are moving in the wrong direction. . . . We surely need to bang the drum and deliver a wake up call. It is so dangerous on the streets, yet funding for the homeless mentally ill (and all the homeless) is being cut back drastically in California—and those streets are dangerous, as witnessed by the latest killing (by gasoline and match) of a depressed man living on Koreatown streets.

We, David's parents, are very aware of how far from the present reality this vision of a better system really is, both in terms of adequate funding and in terms of retraining of service providers. But the first step is to imagine what is needed for a better system. Only then can one begin to work toward making some of that happen. To that end, we are ready to join with other patient advocates, with our local clinic, and with the Los Angeles County mental health system.

Therapy as a specific part of this plan has not yet been discussed. The best recovery therapy, in our view, is through actual accomplishments that build hope and self-esteem. Earning some money and getting concrete counseling on managing this money are more relevant than generalized discussions of money management in a hospital or day program. Taking responsibility to care for one's daily living and taking some steps toward employment are better "therapy" than talking about it in a vacuum.

But this orientation toward self-esteem-building activities does not mean that there is not an essential place for some therapeutic interaction. Both psychiatrists and social workers need to become trusted friends of the person with whom they are working in order to develop a relationship where the person can talk about his or her feelings. Advocates also need to be friends on whom such persons can rely to listen to them as they seek to communicate their concerns. Advocates need to become educated in the nature of mental illness and on their own role, psychologically as well as legally.

An advocate who is a family member—such as a parent, a sibling, or a child—may have dysfunctional relationship patterns with the person for whom they are advocating—angry, fearful, nagging, or authoritarian ways of responding that reflect old conflicts. It is useful to have a therapeutic program designed for advocates to help them sort out these old relationships and find better ways of communicating.

The National Alliance on Mental Illness (NAMI) is already working on some of these needs. It has a course for advocates that provides information on various types of mental illness and on medication. This Family-to-Family Program also offers class exercises on communication skills. In addition, volunteers staff a helpline and go over the information and mail guidelines to those who call in. Where we live, there is a care-and-share group for those with mental illness and their advocates

that meets once a month at the NAMI meetings. Soon there will be
another that meets at the local mental health clinic. About half a dozen
others meet nearby. So, some efforts are under way in this direction, but
more are needed.[8]

People receiving mental health services should be encouraged to
find or develop support groups where they can discuss their experiences, hopes, and needs. Clinics should offer individual and group
therapy that might utilize a mix of therapeutic traditions, including the
techniques of behavioral-cognitive therapy. Therapeutic guidance for
people with mental illness need not be limited to the formal psychiatric settings. Some might seek out a counseling or support relationship through other venues, such as a church, or they might find help
in other religious traditions, such as Buddhist meditation. Underlying
all forms of healing therapy is the personal relationship where someone can really uncover his or her wounds and disappointments and be
helped to move on to a healed self. What needs to be understood is
that recovery from mental illness is not primarily a medical process,
although medications may have a role. It is fundamentally a process of
"soul-cure."

As person-centered therapist Brian Thorne puts it, the important
thing is creating a relationship "where the client can begin to experience
himself or herself as a person of value who is deeply worthy of respect
. . . . [P]erson-centered therapy offers a path along which the client can
travel from self-denigration to self-affirmation, from despair to hope."[9]
Although particular traditions of therapeutic training can offer some
skills in doing that, basically this is about sensitive, compassionate sharing in the context of committed friendship. Those interested in recovery
need to seek out a variety of contexts where they can taste something of
this kind of sharing and supportive relationship.

Spirituality for Recovery

The concluding section of this last chapter will venture a few remarks
about a "spirituality for recovery." By "spirituality" I mean the inner
dynamics of motivation, relationships, values, and meaning. This can

be related to religious traditions, but it need not be tied to any particular one. It is simply the inner dimension of being a thinking, feeling, meaning-seeking human being. Spirituality needs to be discussed
in two contexts: in the context of family or friend advocates of a person
with mental illness, and in the context of the self-understanding of the
person with mental illness. The spirituality of a psychiatrist or a social
worker working with persons with mental illness is not discussed here,
although this could be done by those playing these roles. Mark Ragins,
psychiatrist of the Village, has written about his own understanding of
this for himself.

I have come to understand the relationship between the family
advocate and a person with mental illness to be one of "grace and limits." What I mean by "grace" is that the family advocate (this could also
be a friend, but is most likely a relative of the person) makes a permanent commitment to the person with mental illness. This means making clear to yourself and to the person concerned that, no matter what,
you are not going to abandon that person. No matter how much the
person "messes up," goes through ups and downs, and even becomes
violent or jailed or homeless, you will not give up on the person.

Our commitment to David is concretely an expression of what liberation theology calls a "preferential option for the poor," itself the basic
meaning of a commitment to "life," which must start with those whose
life has been most diminished. Our ongoing commitment to him saves
David from experiencing the raw material poverty into which he would
be plunged without us. But he is surely one of the poor in the way illness has robbed him of much of his human potential. Yet we struggle
every day to help him have some modicum of quality of life, despite his
wounded potential.

This relationship is what might be called, in Christian religious
terms, "unconditional grace." This means that we accept this person
by "grace alone" without regard to any "good works." It does not mean
we don't constantly hope for and encourage the person to do good
works, become better behaved and more hopeful, communicate better,
and start taking responsibility for his or her life. Rather, it means that
the relationship of unconditional grace grounds such good work and

remains in place even when any such good works fail. It is not earned through accomplishments.

It is this relation of unconditional grace that Christians have attributed to God's relation to us. This means that Christians have attributed to God what we have understood as most foundational for human hope and persistence in the struggle for well-being; namely, that we experience the ultimate source of the universe as having unconditional acceptance of us. Hopefully, we each have had some concrete experience of unconditional love in relationships with parents or with a spouse or a committed friend. These are the persons on whom you can count to not let you down or cast you off, no matter what.

But human beings are finite, not infinite. Unconditional commitment needs to be lived out under finite conditions. This means concretely that while you are committed to never abandoning the person, you also do not allow the person to engulf you and take over your life and destroy the possibility of having a life of your own. This is a difficult issue for parents of a person with mental illness. Parents, particularly mothers, have been socialized to give themselves unconditionally to their children and made to feel guilty if they set limits to their domestic responsibilities and insist on having some space for a life of their own.

Our culture still suffers from a bifurcated model of gender roles, with men seen as destined to become the "self-sufficient autonomous adult" and women dedicated to serving men and children unreservedly. Thus, women as wives and particularly as mothers are made to feel guilty if they have not given their whole lives to their children. If children have difficulties, mothers are regularly blamed as the cause of this, particularly if they have also pursued a career. But this model of the "full-time mother" who has no life of her own is as unhealthy as the model of the autonomous male, whose autonomy is actually made possible by the selfless service of others.

What people in relationships—couples and parents—need is a balance of self-care and care for others, a balance between helping others develop their lives and developing their own creative work. This is not a question of creating rigid boundaries between the two; rather, the ability to help others is grounded in caring for our personal self and developing our own creative life and vice versa. In my own experience, relations to others, to members of my family, and to social justice issues constantly nurture and provide the stimulation for my own creative work. This book is a marriage of the two.

Having space for my own work, as well as a safe space for the rest of our family, meant, in earlier periods of David's illness, finding some other places for him to live. So we sought out creative therapeutic communities—Duck Island, Gould Farm, and Kahumana—where David went to live, even as we kept in regular weekly touch with him and visited him periodically. The hope was that separation from the family would help David become independent. That didn't work out. David has proven himself a "homing pigeon" who wants his parents to be his major friends and supporters, who would prefer to live at home with them, rather than in a board-and-care home.

Sending David to Kahumana in Hawaii seemed like a wonderful option at the time. It was also necessary for our psychological survival as a family of two parents and two other siblings. Since the failure of the Hawaii options, these "limits" have been expressed by a commitment bounded by limits of time and place. It is understood that David can't live at home and impinge on our lives 24/7. But we keep on seeking the best place for him to live that we can find, near enough to visit and do things together several times a week. David knows we are there for him and that our commitment to him is unshakeable. But he also knows that he cannot just show up at the house anytime he wants.

Maybe someday he will actually move on to fuller autonomy. Maybe he will not. In any case, he faces a future at some point where we will no longer be there for him. Can he survive that change? Clearly, our present arrangements are fragile and lack long-term viability as we become older and eventually die.

Spirituality for the person with mental illness means not becoming overwhelmed by all that has been lost so that one falls into suicidal depression. It means keeping hope alive. It means starting every day with the sense that something new can happen. We continue to work with David for more "things to do" and better options for daily life that might rebuild hope and steps toward recovery. The other day David, Herman, and I were driving in the car, when David began to sing out the old refrain, "Today is the first day of the rest of your life." The sense that, no matter how much one has lost in the past, one can always start again is key. The future is open. Therapeutic conversation and relationship of the kind discussed earlier is very important in helping those who seek recovery to move beyond self-denigration and despair to self-affirmation and hope.

Occasionally, an acquaintance who, on hearing of David's condition, replies by exclaiming, "Oh, I am so sorry," or "What a tragedy!" This "sorry" response, although well intended, basically treats David as if he is a closed case, as if he is effectively already dead. But David is not dead; he is alive! However diminished from what he might have been (how do we know what he "might have been" except for our fond parental imaginings!), he still has life. He still has potential. He still has hope. In his own words, "I still have hope that life can be interesting." We too need not to lose hope that his life can be interesting.

Significantly, it has been some years since we have received "so sorry" and "what a tragedy" exclamations. Rather, what has become much more common is that the person who hears about David's struggle responds by telling me about his or her own struggle with mental illness or that of a friend or family member. We enter into a useful conversation based on shared experiences. We discover how many people in American society share experiences of mental illness but often are reluctant to discuss them.

For example, while I was printing out the manuscript of this book in the computer lab of my school, a seminarian asked me if I was writing "another book." I said yes, I was writing about the mental health system. I then showed her the table of contents. She quickly replied by saying that her brother is schizophrenic. When I mentioned that I was critiquing the mental health system from our perspective as a family, she responded by saying, "Yes, it is the family that is the prime group that cares about such a person."

In writing this book, I have shared parts of it and, in some cases, the whole manuscript with friends in our community who have children with mental illness. It also has been read by a practicing family therapist and by a professor of pastoral psychology at a theological school, as well as by two doctoral students. More people today know something about mental illness and are no longer afraid to share their own experiences. Sharing your experience often gives permission for them to share theirs.

David's, and our, struggle through the storm to the light continues.

"Returning through the Storm"

Returning through the storm
Across the fields and plains,
Across the roaring sea,
Like a slave,
Whose solemn awareness
Is so filled with ugliness,
His tortured spirit quest.

Returning through the storm,
Across the fields and plains,
Across the roaring sea,
Reaching out for the lost truth.
Another of life's illusions
Yielding to the light.

Returning through the storm,
Across the fields and plains,
Crossing the roaring sea,
Freeing the slave
To relive once more
The colliding stillness
And the picture-puzzle perfection.

Returning through the storm
Across the fields and plains,
Across the roaring sea,
Where you see the shadow
Under the bridge,
As plain as the reflection
In the space where the shadow
Has found its way back to the light.

David Christopher Ruether

Notes

Introduction

1. See Pete Earley, *Crazy: A Father's Search through America's Mental Health Madness* (New York: G. P. Putnam's Sons, 2006), 37–122.

Chapter Two

1. *Diagnostic and Statistical Manual of Mental Disorders* (Washington, D.C.: American Psychiatric Association, 1952), 28.

2. Washington, D.C.: American Psychiatric Association, 2000.

3. Ibid., 306, see also 803, 792, 800, 798, and 795.

4. Ibid., 301.

5. Eugen Bleuler, *Dementia Praecox or the Group of Schizophrenias*, foreword Nolan Lewis (New York: Universities Press, 1950).

6. *DSM-IV-TR*, 299.

7. See article on "REM sleep" in *Wikipedia*, http://en.wikipedia.org/wiki/Rapid-eye-movement-sleep.

8. *Approaching the Qur'an*, introduced and translated by Michael Sells (Ashland, Ore.: White Cloud Press, 2001), 2nd edition, p. 7.

9. Boston: Houghton Mifflin, 1976.

10. Ibid., 100–107.

11. New York: Harper and Brothers, 1936.

12. See Mary Ann Clark, *Santeria: Correcting Myths, Uncovering Realities of a Growing Religion* (New York: Praeger, 2007), passim.

13. Harper Collins, 1995, third edition, pp. 199–120.

14. Matthew McKay, Martha Davis and Patrick Fanning, *Thoughts and Feelings: Taking Control of Your Moods and Your Life* (Oakland, Calif.: New Harbinger Publications, 1997), 27–43.

15. Hyperion, 2007.

16. Among these books by Elyn Saks are *Jekyll on Trial: Multiple Personality Disorder And Criminal Law* (New York: New York University Press, 1997); *Interpreting Interpretation: The Limits of Hermeneutic Psychoanalysis* (New Haven, Conn.: Yale University Press, 1999); and *Refusing Care: Forced Treatment and the Rights of the Mentally Ill* (Chicago: Chicago University Press, 2002).

17. See especially the writing of E. Fuller Torrey who is extremely hostile to psychoanalysis. See his *Freudian Fraud: The Malignant Effects of Freud's Theory on American Thought and Culture* (New York: HarperPerennial, 1993).

Chapter Three

1. "The Humors," http://georgetowncollege.edu/english/allen/humors.htm.

2. See G. J. Barker-Benfield, *The Horrors of the Half-Known Life: Male Attitudes toward Women and Sexuality in Nineteenth Century America* (San Francisco: Harper and Row, 1976), 163–174.

3. Gerald N. Grob, *The Mad Among Us: A History of the Care of America's Mentally Ill* (New York: The Free Press, 1994), 28.

4. Ibid., 26.

5. Ibid., 28–29. Samuel Tuke, *Description of the Retreat, an Institution near York for the Insane of the Society of Friends, Containing an Account of Its Origins and Progress, the Modes of Treatment and a Statement of Cases* (Philadelphia: Isaac Peirce, 1813).

6. See Donald J. Rothman, *The Discovery of Asylum: Social Order and Disorder in the New Republic* (Boston: Little, Brown, 1971), 3–27.

7. Grob, *The Mad Among Us*, 27.

8. Gerald N. Grob, *The Mentally Ill in America: A History of their Care and Treatment From Colonial Times*, 2nd edition (New York: Colombia University Press, 1949),

9. Kraepelin's writings have been edited in seven volumes. Wolfgang Burgmair, Eric J. Engstorm and Matthias Weber, et al., eds. *Emil Kraeplin*, 7 vols. (Munich: Belleville, 2000–2008).

10. Gerald N. Grob, *Mental Illness and American Society, 1875–1940* (Princeton, N.J.: Princeton University Press, 1983), 110–112.

11. For a book-length study of the life and work of Henry Cotton, see Andrew Scull, *Madhouse: A Tragic Tale of Megalomania and Modern Medicine* (New Haven, Conn.: Yale University Press, 2005).

12. See Robert Whitaker, *Mad in America: Bad Science, Bad Medicine and the Enduring Mistreatment of the Mentally Ill* (Cambridge, Mass.: Perseus Books, 2002), 73–106.

13. See Jack El-Hai, *The Lobotomist: A Maverick Genius and His Tragic Quest to Rid the World of Mental Illness* (New York: John Wiley and Son, 2005), especially chpt. 10.

14. See Grob, *The Mad Among Us*, 143. Adolph Meyer, born in Switzerland in 1886 and trained in neurology, was seen as the dean of American psychiatry from the 1890s to his retirement on the eve of World War II. He was head of the psychiatric clinic of Johns Hopkins University from 1910 to 1941. A good exposition of his thought is Eunice E. Winters and Anna Mae Bowers, *Psychobiology: A Science of Man* (Springfield, Ill.: Charles C. Thomas, 1957).

15. Freud's major works are found in the *Standard Edition of the Complete Psychological Words of Sigmund Freud* (London: Hogarth Press, 1953). For a brief overview of Freud's view of the psychological construction of gender, see Rosemary Ruether, *New Woman, New Earth: Sexist Ideologies and Human Liberation* (Boston: Beacon Press, 1995), 138–140.

16. For example, Walter Freeman, leading promoter of lobotomy as the cure for mental illness was enraged by the dominance of Freudian theory in departments of psychiatry in universities. E. Fuller Torrey, popular authority on schizophrenia remains very hostile to Freud; see his *Freudian Fraud: The Malignant Effect of Freud's Theories on American Thought and Culture* (New York: Harper Collins, 1993).

17. Revised edition: *The Myth of Mental Illness: Foundations of a Theory of Personal Conduct* (New York: Harper and Row, 1974).

18. Foucault's *Madness and Civilization: A History of Insanity in an Age of Reason* (New York: Pantheon, 1965) was published as an abridged version of *Folie et déraison: Histoire de la folie á l'âge classique*, originally published in 1961. Foucault's second major book, *The Birth of the Clinic: An Archaeology of Medical Perception* (New York: Pantheon), was published in French in 1963 and translated into English in 1973.

19. R. D. Laing, *The Divided Self: An Existential Study in Sanity and Madness* (Harmondsworth: Penguin, 1960) and *Sanity, Madness, and the Family* (London: Penguin, 1964).

20. For a very unsympathetic view of the ex-patient movement, see Rael Jean Isaac and Virginia C. Armat, *Madness in the Streets: How Psychiatry and the Law Abandoned the Mentally Ill* (New York: The Free Press, 1990), 163–176. For the perspective of the ex-patient movement, see Sherry Hirsch, ed., *Madness Network New Reader* (San Francisco: Glide Publications, 1974).

21. A hostile view of the Mental Health Bar that defended the human rights of the mentally ill is found in Isaac and Armat, *Madness in the Streets*, 107–160. A leader of the Mental Health Bar is Bruce Ennis; see his *Prisoners of Psychiatry: Mental Patients, Psychiatrists and the Law* (New York: Harcourt Brace Jovanovich, 1972).

22. This term was first used in F. Fromm-Reichmann, *Psychoanalysis and Psychotherapy* (Chicago: Chicago University Press, 1959), 164.

23. For the history of the development of Chlorpromazine, see Judith P. Swazey, *Chlorpromazine in Psychiatry: A Study of Therapeutric Innovation* (Cambridge, Mass.: MIT Press, 1974).

24. Whitaker, *Mad in America*, 141–146.

25. "President Seeks Funds to Reduce Mental Illness," *New York Times*, February 6, 1963. On the marketing makeover of Thorazine, see Whitaker, *Mad in America*, 147–155.

26. Whitaker, *Mad in America*, 162–164.

27. Ibid., 195–198.

28. See essay by Susan Kembler, in Colin Ross and Alvin Pam, eds., *Pseudoscience in Biological Psychiatry* (New York: John Wiley and Sons, 1995), 246.

29. E. Fuller Torrey, *Surviving Schizophrenia: A Manual for Families, Consumers and Providers*, 3rd edition. (New York: Harper Collins, 1995), 158.

30. Ibid., 167.

31. This article in the *Archives of General Psychiatry* appeared August 5, 2008, and was reported in Denise Gellene, "Psychotherapy Increasingly Takes a Backseat to Pills, Study Finds," *Los Angeles Times* (Aug. 5, 2008): A9.

32. This statement reflects our own experience over thirty years with dozens of psychiatrists prescribing medication to David.

33. See Herb Kutchins and Stuart Kirk, *Making Us Crazy: DSM: The Psychiatrist's Bible and the Creation of Mental Disorders* (New York: The Free Press, 1997), 205. This remark by Calhoun appeared in "Reflections on the Census of 1840" in *Southern Literary Messenger* 9 (June 1843), 350, cited in Kutchins and Kirk.

34. See Richard Hofstadter, *Social Darwinism in American Thought* (New York: George Braziller, 1959).

35. See section on the United States, in the *Wikipedia* article "Compulsory Sterilization," http://en.wikipedia.org/wiki/Compulsory_sterilization, 1–3.

36. Whitaker, *Mad in America*, 58.

37. Ibid., 60; see also Ian Robert Dowbiggen, *Keeping America Sane: Psychiatry and Eugenics in the U.S. and Canada: 1880–1940* (Ithaca, N.Y.: Cornell University Press, 1997) and *The Sterilization Movement and Global Fertility, The Twentieth Century* (Oxford: Oxford University Press, 2008).

38. See Joel Braslow, *Mental Ills and Bodily Cures: Psychiatric Treatment in the First Half of the Twentieth Century* (Berkeley: The University of California, 1997), 61–68.

39. See Paul Weindling, "The Rockefeller Foundation and German Biomedical Sciences, 1920–1940," in Nicolas Rupke, ed., *Science, Politics and the Public Good* (New York: Macmillan, 1988), 119–140.

40. Whitaker, *Mad in America*, 142.

41. Irving Gottesman, *Schizophrenia Genesis: The Origins of Madness* (New York: W. H. Freeman, 1991), continually cites F. Kallman, German immigrant to the United States for the reliability of his genetic studies of mental illness, despite his roots in early Nazi research to promote sterilization of the mentally ill. This is severely critiqued by Alvin Pam, "Biological Psychiatry: Science or Pseudoscience" in *Pseudoscience in Biological Psychiatry* (New York: John Wiley and Sons, 1995), 14–17.

42. See particularly Gottesman, *Schizophrenia Genesis*, 82–132, for the studies on inheritance of mental illness. A brief summary of the statistics is found in Torrey, *Surviving Schizophrenia*, 314.

43. Ross and Pam, eds., *Pseudoscience in Biological Psychiatry*, 35.

44. Assen Jablensky, "Schizophrenia: Manifestations, Incidence and Course in Different Countries, a World Health Organization Ten-Country Study," *Psychological Medicine*, Supplement 20 (1992):1–95.

45. (New York: Bantam, 2001).

46. The Inverness-based research group, Food and Behavior Research, www.fabresearch.org, pursues research on the relation of diet and both mental and physical health, and particularly promotes including oily fish and omega-3 fatty acids in the diet. The dietary supplement Kirunal is a source of such fatty acids. The Key Company in St. Louis promotes Kirunal as "providing nutritional help for schizophrenia, bipolar disorder and severe simple depression."

47. Charles Barber, *Comfortably Numb: How Psychiatry Is Medicating a Nation* (New York: Pantheon, 2008), 155.

48. Ibid., 257, esp. notes 24 and 25.

49. Chris Harrop and Peter Trower, *Why Does Schizophrenia Develop at Late Adolescence? A Cognitive-Developmental Approach to Psychosis* (New York: John Wiley and Sons, 2003).

50. Ibid., 14, 16.

51. Kutchins and Kirk, *Making Us Crazy*, 100–125. In the *DSM-IV-TR* 2000 edition, PTSD appears on pp. 463–468.

52. The literature on PTSD is extensive and growing. Two useful studies are *Psychobiology of Post-traumatic Stress Disorder: A Decade of Progress*, Rachel Yehuda, ed. (Boston: Blackwell, 2006) and Michael J. Scott, *Moving on After Trauma: A Guide for Survivors, Family and Friends* (New York: Routledge, 2008).

53. See Kutchins and Kirk, *Making Us Crazy*, 118, 125.

194 Notes

54. See Jeffrey M. Masson, *The Assault on Truth: Freud's Suppression of the Seduction Theory* (New York: Farrar, Straus and Giroux, 1984).
55. Eric R. Kandel, *The Search of Memory: The Emergence of a New Science of Mind* (New York: Norton, 2006).
56. Quoted in Barber, *Comfortably Numb*, 194.
57. *American Journal of Psychiatry* 155 (April, 1998), 457–469.
58. Quoted in Barber, *Comfortably Numb*, 195, see note 13 on page 263. Norman Doidge develops this interactive approach in his book, *The Brain That Changes Itself: Stories of Personal Triumph from the Frontiers of Brain Science* (New York: Viking, 2007).
59. See Emma Young, "Strange Inheritance: It's not just your parents' genes but also their experiences that determine your genetic makeup," *New Scientist*, July 12–18, 2008, 29–33.
60. See Barber, *Comfortably Numb*, 200.
61. See David K. Sakheim and Susan E. Devine, "Trauma-Related Symptoms" and Colin A. Ross, "Conclusion: A Trauma Model" in Ross and Pam, eds., *Pseudoscience in Biological Psychiatry*, 255–278.
62. Quoted in Barber, *Comfortably Numb*, 201.

Chapter Four

1. See NAMI "StigmaBusters" on the Web at http://www.nami.org/template.cfm?section=fight_stigma.
2. NAMI: "The VTI Tragedy: Distinguishing Mental Illness from Violence," http://www.nami.org/Template.cfm?Section=press_room&template=/ContentManagement/ContentDisplay.cfm&ContentID=45417 (accessed June 16, 2008).
3. See particularly Charles Barber, *Comfortably Numb: Medicating the Nation* (New York: Pantheon, 2008).
4. Lynn Gamwell and Nancy Tomes, *Madness in America: The Cultural and Medical Perceptions of Mental Illness before 1914* (Binghamton, N.Y.: SUNY Press, 1995), 38.
5. Thomas Morton, *The History of the Pennsylvania Hospital* (Times Printing House, 1895), 163, cited in Robert Whitaker, *Mad in America: Bad Science, Bad Medicine and the Enduring Mistreatment of the Mentally Ill* (Cambridge, Mass.: Perseus Books, 2002), 4.
6. Ibid., 5.
7. See Bethlem Royal Hospital, *Wikipedia*, http://en.wikipedia.org/wiki/Bethlem_Royal_Hospital.
8. Whitaker, *Mad in America*, 6.
9. See Ida Macalpine and Richard Hunter, *George III and the Mad Business* (New York: Penguin, 1969), 47–86.
10. Ibid., 172–175.
11. Ibid., 131–171.
12. Ibid., 347–353.
13. For a picture of this "tranquilizing chair," see Gamwell and Tomes, *Madness in America*, 33.
14. For pictures of such restraints, see Ibid., 46–47.
15. For two images of such cribs, Ibid., 48–49.
16. The policy of nonrestraint was actually started by an assistant, Robert Gardiner Hill, with Connolly taking credit for the changed policy: See Andrew Scull, *Social Order/Mental Disorder: Anglo-American Psychiatry in Historical Perspective* (Berkeley: University of California, 1989), 193–195.
17. Ibid., 46; See also Albert Deutsch, *The Mentally Ill in America: A History of Their Care and Treatment from Colonial Times* (New York: Columbia University Press, 1945), chpt. 11.
18. Elyn Saks, *The Center Cannot Hold* (New York: Hyperion, 2007), is the personal biography of her experience of illness and treatment in England and the United States.
19. Elyn Saks, *Refusing Care: Forced Treatment and the Rights of the Mentally Ill* (Chicago: University of Chicago Press, 2002), 146–172.
20. Ibid., 245. See her numerous references in note 3.
21. Whitaker, *Mad in America*, 11–12; also Scull, *Social Order/Mental Disorder*, 69–70.
22. Whitaker, *Mad in America*, 75–77. Joel Braslow, *Mental Ills and Bodily Cures* (Berkeley: University of California Press, 1997), 47–50.
23. Braslow, *Mental Ills and Bodily Cures*, 43–50.
24. Ibid., 37, 104–111 and passim.
25. See Scull, *Social Order/Mental Disorder*, 71–80.

26. Gamwell and Tomes, 32: Whitaker, *Mad in America*, 13–15; also Benjamin Rush, *Medical Inquiries and Observations upon the Diseases of the Mind* (Hanger Publishing Company, 1962, reprint of the 1912 edition).

27. Whitaker, *Mad in America*, 82–83.

28. Tonse N. K. Raju, "Hot Brains: Manipulating Body Heat to Save the Brain" from *Pediatrics* online, vol. 117, no. 2 (February 2006), 320–321 (http://pediatrics.aappublications.org/cgi/content/full/117/2/e320).

29. For malaria fever as a cure particularly for paresis, see Joel Braslow, *Mental Ills and Bodily Cures*, 71–94.

30. Ibid., 84–89.

31. Whitaker, *Mad in America*, 92–96.

32. Braslow, *Mental Ills and Bodily Cures*, 97.

33. Ibid., 85–89.

34. See Peter Breggin, *Brain-Disabling Treatments in Psychiatry: Drugs, Electroshock and the Psychopharmaceutical Complex* (New York: Springer, 2008), 217–251, for contemporary use of electroshock.

35. For an overview see "Electroconvulsive Therapy," *Wikipedia*, http://en.wikipedia.org/wiki/Electroconvulsive_therapy (accessed June 18, 2008).

36. Cited in Braslow, *Mental Ills and Bodily Cures*, 103–104.

37. Ibid., 103.

38. Philpot M. Collins, et al, "Eliciting Users' Views of ECT," *Journal of Mental Health* 13 (4): 403–413, 2004.

39. Kitty Dukakis and L. Tye, from "I Feel Good, I Feel Alive," *Newsweek* (September 18, 2006): 62–63, http://www.newsweek.com/id/45609/page/1; also her book, *Shock: The Healing Power of Electroconvulsive Therapy* (New York: Penguin, 2006).

40. A.E. Hotchner, *Papa Hemingway: A Personal Memoir*, (New York: Random House, 1966), 280.

41. Jack El-Hai, *The Lobotomist: A Maverick Medical Genius and His Tragic Quest to Rid the World of Mental Illness* (New York: John Wiley and Sons, 2005), 9.

42. Ibid., 13.

43. For different evaluations of the positive effects of lobotomy, see Elliot S. Valenstein, *Great and Desperate Cures; The Rise and Decline of Psychosurgery and Other Radical Treatments of Mental Illness* (New York: Basic, 1986), who takes a more critical view, and Jack D. Pressman, *Last Resort: Psychosurgery and the Limits of Medicine* (Cambridge: Cambridge University Press, 1998), who is more defensive toward it as reflecting the experimental nature of medicine.

44. El-Hai, *The Lobotomist*, 171.

45. Whitaker, *Mad in America*, 126, citing from Walter Freeman's own reports on the outcomes of his operations in his book, Walter Freeman and James Watt, *Psychosurgery* (Springfield, Ill.: Charles C. Thomas, 1950), 226–257.

46. Rosemary could do math and is estimated to have had an IQ of 90. In 1994 her diaries from 1936–1938 came to light, preserved by her mother's secretary. These writing show a lively young women interested in tea dances, dress fittings, and visits to Europe and to the White House; see Graeme Zielinski, "Life Outside the Sportlight," *Milwaukee Journal Sentinel OnLine*, (Jan. 9, 2005), http://www.jsonline.com/.

47. The exception is Eunice Kennedy, who went to Stanford. Kathleen, Patricia, and Jean all graduated from Catholic women's schools. All four Kennedy sons went to Harvard.

48. Lawrence Leamer, *The Kennedy Women: The Saga of an American Family* (New York: Villard Books, 1994), 319.

49. Ibid., 322.

50. Ibid.

51. Ibid., 322–323; also El-Hai, *The Lobotomist*, 173–174.

52. In an interview with Ronald Kessler, Watts stated that, in his opinion, Rosemary suffered from some kind of depression. See http://www.newsmax.com/kessler.Rosemary_Kennedy/2008/06/17/105127.html.

53. Braslow, *Mental Ills, Bodily Cures*, 152–170.

54. Ibid., 165–168.

55. Ibid., 174.

56. E. Fuller Torrey, *Surviving Schizophrenia* (New York: Harper Perennial, 1995), 192.

57. JoEllen Patterson, A. Ari Albala, Margaret E. McCahill, and Todd M. Edwards, *The Therapist's Guide to Psychopharmacology: Working with Patients, Families, and Physicians to Optimize Care* (New York: Guilford, 2006), 125.

58. Torrey, *Surviving Schizophrenia*, 193.

59. Ibid.

60. "Peter Breggin," *Wikipedia*, http://en.wikipedia.org/wiki/Peter_Breggin.

61. Peter Breggin, *Toxic Psychiatry: Why Therapy, Empathy and Love Must Replace the Drugs, Electroshock and Biochemical Theories of the "New Psychiatry"* (New York: St. Martin's, 1991); Peter Breggin, *Talking Back to Prozac: What Doctors Won't Tell You about Today's Most Controversial Drug* (New York: St. Martin's, 1999); Peter Breggin, *Talking Back to Ritalin: What Doctors Won't Tell You about Stimulants for Children* (Monroe, Maine: Common Courage Press, 1998); Peter Breggin, *The Heart of Being Helpful: Empathy and the Creation of a Healing Presence* (New York: Springer, 1997); Peter Breggin with David Cohen, *Your Drug May Be Your Problem: How and Why to Stop Taking Psychiatric Medications*, (Reading, Mass.: Oxford, 1999); Peter Breggin, *Brain-Disabling Treatments in Psychiatry: Drugs, Electroshock and the Psychopharmaceutical Complex* (New York: Springer, 2008).

62. Breggin, *Toxic Psychiatry*, 92–108.

63. Ibid., 24–46.

64. Anton Boisen, *The Exploration of the Inner World: A Study of Mental Disorder and Religious Experience* (New York: Harper and Brothers, 1936), 15–122.

65. Ibid., 53–54, 56.

66. Ibid., 84–85.

67. Such as Robert Whitaker, author of *Mad in America*.

68. See report on Libermann's remarks at the Fourth Annual Palm Beach symposium in *NARSAD Research Quarterly*, vol. 1/3 (Fall/Winter 2008) 27–28.

69. The information on these companies and their neuroleptic products was drawn from the Internet, first by looking up the drugs and finding out who produces them and then looking up the companies.

70. See Stanley Wohl, *The Medical Industrial Complex* (New York: Harmony Books, 1984). See also Marcia Angell, *The Truth about the Drug Companies: How They Deceive Us and What to Do about Them* (New York: Random House, 2004).

71. Steven Scharfstein, "Psychosocial Treatments, We Owe It to Our Patients," in *Psychiatric News* (March 3, 2006): 3.

72. See Breggin, *Toxic Psychiatry*, 344–352. Also Angell, *The Truth about the Drug Companies*, 208–214.

73. See G. Harris, "At F.D.A., Strong Drug Ties and Less Monitoring," *The New York Times* (Dec. 6, 2004): 1.

74. Breggin, *Brain-Disabling Treatments*, 350–369. See also Breggin, "On the FDA and Drug Companies," in *Toxic Psychiatry*, 361–362.

75. Breggin, *Brain-Disabling Treatments*, 373.

76. Available on NIHM Web site, http://www.nihm.hih.gov.

77. On for-profit research companies paid for by the drug companies, see Angell, *The Truth about the Drug Companies*, 100–114, 156–172.

78. See the critique of drug testing and journal articles in Whitaker, *Mad in America*, 253–286.

79. Angell, *The Truth about the Drug Companies*, 138–141.

80. Breggin, *Toxic Psychiatry*, 364–365.

81. New York: The Free Press, 1997.

82. See Christopher Lane, *Shyness: How Normal Behavior Became a Sickness* (New Haven, Conn.: Yale University Press, 2007).

83. See especially Breggin, *Talking Back to Ritalin*.

84. See article by Ron Grossman, "Psychiatry Manual's Secrecy Criticized," *L.A. Times* (Dec. 29, 2008): A19, http://www.latimes.com/features/la-na-mental-disorders29-2008dec29,0,3923115.story. Also Christopher Lane, "Wrangling over Psychiatry's Bible," *L.A. Times* (Nov. 16, 2008), http://latimes.com/news/opinion/commentary/la-oe-lane16-2008Nov16,0,5678764.story, and Robert L Spitzer, "Making the Making of DSM-V Transparent," in *Pasadena Therapist* (Nov. 26, 2008), http://pasadenatherapist.wordpress.com/2008/11/26/making-the-making-of-dsm-v-transparent.

85. For Breggin's critique of NAMI, see his *Toxic Psychiatry*, 362–363.

Chapter Five

1. Braintree, Massachusetts, town records, 1640–1703, p. 26, cited in Albert Deutsch, *The Mentally Ill in America: A History of Their Care and Treatment from Colonial Times* (New York: Columbia University Press, 1945), 42.

2. E. Fuller Torrey, *Surviving Schizophrenia: A Manual for Families, Consumers and Providers* (New York: HarperCollins, 1995), 11.

3. Deutsch, *The Mentally Ill in America*, 117–120.

4. Torrey, *Surviving Schizophrenia*, 10

5. See "Why Skid Row Has Become L.A.'s Dumping Ground," *Los Angeles Times* (October 5, 2005), http://articles.latimes.com/2005/oct/05/local/me-dumping5.

6. David Wagner, *The Poorhouse: America's Forgotten Institution* (Lanham, Md.: Rowman & Littlefield, 2005), 2.

7. Ibid., 10, 14.

8. "Report of the Commissioners on the subject of the Pauper System of the Commonwealth of Massachusetts, 1833," House of Representatives Documents, 1833, No. 6. p. 44, cited in Deutsch, *The Mentally Ill in America*, 129–130.

9. New York State Assembly documents, 1839, vol. 6, no. 310, 11–15: cited in Deutsch, *The Mentally Ill in America*, 130.

10. Wagner, *The Poorhouse*, 27–31.

11. Ibid., 131–150.

12. Deutsch, *The Mentally Ill in America*, 88–92, 95.

13. See Anne Digby, *Madness, Morality and Medicine: A Study of the York Retreat, 1796–1914* (Cambridge, Mass.: Cambridge University Press, 1985).

14. Ibid., 105–39, 237–258.

15. http://theretreatyork.org.uk/abouttheteat.php.

16. "Memorial of D. L. Dix, Praying a grant of land for the relief and support of the indigent Insane in the U.S., June 27, 1848" (U.S. Senate, *Miscellaneous Documents*, No. 150), cited in Deutsch, *The Mentally Ill in America*, 177.

17. Ibid., 184, 185.

18. Gerald N. Grob, *Mental Illness and American Society, 1875–1940* (Princeton, N.J.: Princeton University Press, 1983), 8, 11.

19. For a comparison to the similar style of architecture in England, see Andrew Scull, "Moral Architecture: The Victorian Lunatic Asylum," in *Social Order/Mental Disorder: Anglo-American Psychiatry in Historical Perspective* (Berkeley: University of California Press), 213–238.

20. The classic presentation of the therapeutic system of classification and how patients responded to it is Erving Goffman, *Asylums* (New York: Anchor Books, 1961), 171–320.

21. Grob, *Mental Illness*, 15–29.

22. Andrew Scull, *Madhouse: A Tragic Tale of Megalomania and Modern Medicine* (New Haven, Conn.: Yale University Press, 2005).

23. Erving Goffman, *Asylums*, 171–320.

24. Gerald N. Grob, *The Mad among Us: A History of the Care of America's Mentally Ill* (New York: The Free Press, 1994), 268–278.

25. Albert Deutsch, *The Mentally Ill in America: A History of their Care and Treatment from Colonial Times* (New York: Columbia University Press, 1945), 41.

26. New York: Arno, 1948, reprint 1973.

27. Grob, *The Mad among Us*, 210–220.

28. Ibid., 253.

29. *Mental Health: A Report of the Surgeon General*, chpt. 2, http://www.surgeongeneral.gov/library/mentalhealth/chapter2/sec7.html (accessed Sept. 13, 2009).

30. Ibid.

31. "Community Mental Health Services Block Grant Program," http://mentalhealth.samhsa.gov/publications/allpubs/KEN95-0022/ (accessed Sept. 13, 2009).

32. Grob, *The Mad among Us*, 266

33. Ibid., 267.

34. Ibid., 290.

35. Ibid., 290.

36. See "Supplemental Security Income," *Wikipedia,* http://en.wikipedia.orp/wiki/Supplemental_ Security_Income (accessed Feb. 4, 2008).

37. See Ann Braden Johnson, *Out of Bedlam: The Truth about Deinstitutionalization* (New York: Basic Books, 1992), 120–125.

38. Deutsch, *The Mentally Ill in America*, 41.

39. See Wagner, *The Poorhouse*, 4–6

40. See Terence Thornberry and Joseph E. Jacoby, *The Criminally Insane: A Community Follow-up of Mentally Ill Offenders* (Chicago: The University of Chicago Press, 1979).

41. Johnson, *Out of Bedlam*, 62–67.

42. *Portland Herald Press* (Jan. 13, 2002), and *The Los Angeles Times* (Nov. 20, 2001).

43. See "Criminalization of Individuals with Severe Psychiatric Disorders," http://www.Treatmentadvocacycenter.org/GeneralResources/Fact3.htm (accessed July 2, 2008).

44. This is based on a 2004 survey of State and Federal correctional institutions and a 2002 survey of local jails; see http://www.ncjrs.gov/App/Publications/abstract.aspx?ID=235099.

45. For a personal story of the criminalization of the mentally ill and their deplorable treatment in the Miami-Dade County Pre-Trial Detention Center, see Pete Earley, *Crazy: A Father's Search through America's Mental Health Madness* (New York: C.P. Putnam's Sons, 2006).

46. Torrey, *Surviving Schizophrenia*, 3.

47. In May 2008 the Pomona Valley chapter of NAMI heard a talk by a police officer of the Claremont, California, Police Department detailing this developing sophistication in the treatment of the mentally ill by their police.

48. New York: The Free Press, 1990, 107–160

49. See Deutsch, *The Mentally Ill in America*, 418–424.

50. Ibid., 424–426.

51. Ibid., 427–441.

52. See Bruce Ennis, *Prisoners of Psychiatry* (New York: Harcourt, Brace and Jovanovich, 1972).

53. See California Association of Mental Health Patient's Rights Advocates, http://camhpra.org.

54. Ibid., *Manual of Patient's Rights*, chpt. 9.

55. See Anton Boisen, *Hymns of Hope and Courage: A Service Book for Use in Hospitals* (Chicago: Chicago Theological Seminary, 1950); see also Boisen's *Exploration of the Inner World: A Study of Mental Disorder and Religion* (New York: Harpers and Brothers, 1936), 255–259.

Chapter Six

1. All this information is taken from the Gould Farm Web site, http://www.newfarm.org/features/ ll04/gould/index.shtml, as well as an article by Dan Sullivan, "Farming for Health and Wellbeing," Rodale Institute (November 23, 2004).

2. http://www.kahumana.org/TherapeuticLivingProgram.php.

3. http://thresholds.org/home2.asp.

4. Mark Ragins, *A Road to Recovery* (Los Angeles: Mental Health Association of Los Angeles County, 2002), 2.

5. Ibid., 37.

6. Ibid., 50.

7. See Beth Baker, *Old Age in a New Age: The Promise of Transformative Nursing Homes* (Nashville: Vanderbilt University, 2007).

8. I thank Dick Bunce for this comment.

9. Brian Thorne, "Spiritual Intelligence and the Person-Centered Therapist," in Jonathan Baxter, ed., *Wounds that Heal: Theology, Imagination and Health* (London: SPCK, 2007), 226.

Index